THE WARNING SIGNS

You may be a casualty in a losing battle against credit card debt if you recognize yourself in any of the following:

- You are paying the minimum or less each month
- Your balances are increasing every month
- Your monthly expenses are higher than your monthly income
- You are no longer paying attention to the amount you owe
- You are no longer able to maintain a savings account
- You don't use cash; you pay for everything with credit cards, including other credit cards
- You had to cut other important monthly expenses in order to pay the minimum on your credit card
- Your heartbeat increases every time your credit card is run through the cashier's machine, in fear that you have passed your limit

**IF YOU FIT ANY OF THESE PROFILES
THIS BOOK IS FOR YOU!**

CREDIT CARD DEBT

REDUCE YOUR FINANCIAL
BURDEN IN THREE EASY STEPS

DISCARDED

ALEXANDER DASKALOFF

AVON BOOKS   JAN 0 2 2003
An Imprint of HarperCollinsPublishers

I would like to thank all those involved in making this book possible. Special thanks goes to Stacey Donovan for her invaluable help in editing and to Mara Covell and Peter Winslow for their intuitive ideas and suggestions.

AVON BOOKS
An Imprint of HarperCollins*Publishers*
10 East 53rd Street
New York, New York 10022-5299

Copyright © 1999 by Alexander Daskaloff
Published by arrangement with the author
Library of Congress Catalog Card Number: 98-94812
ISBN: 0-380-80700-9
www.avonbooks.com

This book is dedicated to my parents Nadine and Gyorgy.

Contents

✔A check mark has been placed in front of those sections containing the fastest and surest ways to reduce credit card debt for those who require the suggestions and recommendations in this book but lack the time to study all chapters.

Introduction

> *The most common man-made material is plastic. It
> makes you wonder if credit cards have anything to do
> with it . . .*
>
> —A CREDIT CARD CONSUMER

*Credit Card Debt . . . Reduce Your Financial Burden in
Three Easy Steps* is a unique guide designed to significantly reduce the burden and cost of your credit card debt. Credit cards have become a major part of our everyday lives, and
with almost everyone we know using them in the United
States, they've almost become a necessary evil in our society.

Evil or not, credit cards are so overused by so many consumers that the singular aspect of dependence upon them
can probably explain the current national $450 billion in
credit card debt and the average 17% interest paid on those
debts. Whose fault is this? Some argue that it's the consumer's, while other say the fault belongs with the issuers of
credit cards.

Whatever the reason, it's important for the consumer to
take immediate action. Chances are you've been overburdened by credit card debt as a result of loss of income, an
unexpected obligation, or a sudden change of lifestyle. Perhaps you simply purchased some major items or found yourself relying on your credit cards to pay more and more

incoming bills. It might even be true that your dependence on them has been minimal and you've just been following the issuer's rules and guidelines in handling your growing debt.

There are many possible reasons, but whatever the circumstance, this book will provide you with new guidelines, new techniques, and numerous suggestions that, once taken, will ultimately free you from your credit card debt. You will soon make your own rules, rather than follow the rules set forth by the credit card companies! Think of this book as a key; with it, you will learn to unlock the door to credit card freedom.

Credit Card Debt . . . has been divided into three parts and can be read in one of several ways, since certain sections will have more relevance to some readers than to others. However, I do recommend reading from beginning to end, not only to ultimately reduce your credit card debt, but to gather as much financial information as possible.

"Part One: The Road to Freedom" is designed so that you can quickly organize, analyze, and ultimately reduce your credit card debt.

- ✂ "Organizing," the first section, deals with placing information about your credit card debt onto several charts, which will help you stay organized throughout the rest of the book.
- ✂ "Analyzing," the second section, is where you begin analyzing the information on those charts, including the flexibility of your debt, how much it is costing you, and the credit cards that need to be dealt with first.
- ✂ "Reducing," the final section, combines the work from the previous two sections into reducing the cost of your debt by transferring balances, calling the credit card companies for lower interest rates, and planning ahead for sneaky credit card traps and tricks.

"Part Two: A Few Signs on the Highway" delves into further detail toward understanding the unique aspects of credit cards.

- ✂ "What You Need to Know" explains why you should not automatically pay the minimum payment due as required by the credit cards, how to escape paying the annual fee, increasing your credit limit so that more of your debt is owed at a lower rate, how interest rates are calculated, and the proper use of a cash advance.

- ✂ "The Plastic" provides information on the credit card in general: why credit cards are valuable to consumers, the different types of credit cards available, how credit card issuers determine risky consumers, why the business is so profitable, and some interesting statistics on credit card debt in the United States.

- ✂ "What You *Might* Want to Know," deals with what the consumer should do if he or she is still heavily burdened by credit card debt. Many alternative methods are mentioned here, including living on a budget, consolidating debts, looking for other unique choices, and even filing for bankruptcy.

"Part Three: Your Final Destination" provides additional information about what the consumer should know about their credit cards in addition to managing their credit card debt.

- ✂ "Better Safe . . . Than Sorry" explains how the consumer can be protected through the use of credit cards. Checking one's credit history, appropriate safety guidelines when using credit cards, and knowing one's rights if something goes wrong are included.

- ✂ "Some Final Comments" provides a quick wrap-up of what was presented throughout the book. There is a review section, suggestions on how to avoid additional credit card debt, and even how to access further up-to-the-minute information through my unique Internet Web Site.

At the end of the book you'll find a glossary, a sample statement, and also a diagram of the credit card to prove that its not just plastic.

Remember, it can be a never-ending battle between you and the credit card, especially if you follow the rules and guidelines of the credit card issuer. It's in their best interest for you to stay in debt as long as possible. For many people, the credit card has unfortunately become a necessary evil. However, for those who have been trapped and tricked by credit cards, things are about to change. Just follow the steps and suggestions provided by this book and you will significantly reduce your credit card debt. So buckle up as you head out onto the road to financial freedom!

Credit Card Debt . . .

Reduce Your

Financial Burden in

Three Easy Steps

The Interactive Edition

Are You a Victim?

THE WARNING SIGNS

Welcome to the world of credit cards, a very profitable business for those who issue them and the most deceiving type of available loan to those who use them. Chances are, you or someone you know is a casualty of credit card debt. The battle to get out of credit card debt can be never-ending, especially without the proper guidance. But in order to find out if you are truly a casualty in a losing battle, you must see if any of the following situations portray the relationship between you and your credit card.

SOUND FAMILIAR?

- ✂ You are paying the minimum or less each month.
- ✂ Your balances are increasing every month.
- ✂ Your monthly expenses are higher than your monthly income.
- ✂ You are no longer paying attention to the amount you owe.
- ✂ You are no longer able to maintain a savings account.
- ✂ You no longer use cash; instead you pay everything with credit cards and are even using cash advance checks to pay your expenses, including other credit cards.

3

✂ You had to cut other important monthly expenses in order to pay the minimums on your credit cards.

✂ You do not open your mail for fear that one of the letters could be from one of your credit card issuers.

✂ Your heartbeat increases every time the credit card is run through the cashier's machine in the hope that you have not passed your card limit.

If any of these items match your relationship with credit cards, there are two simple steps you can take:

1. Read this book! It is the most important step you can make in defeating your credit card debt!
2. Stop using your credit cards (the final use of your credit card should have been the purchase of this book).

It's that simple.

WHAT LIES AHEAD

What lies ahead is the ammunition you need to win the battle against credit card debt. If you win the battle does it mean you've won the war? Winning the war is up to you. What this book offers is step-by-step procedures in organizing, analyzing, and reducing your debt. Continuing to use the skills you learn from these pages is all the artillery you'll need.

Like many others, you've probably been following the rules issued by your credit card companies, and by doing so, your debt is taking forever to end. *Credit Card Debt . . .* will help you put those same rules to work for *you*, rather than for the credit card companies.

Remember that this book is on your side and that as long

as you follow its procedures, you will lower your costs and finally be relieved of credit card debt! No matter how you became indebted—whether you lost a job, got divorced, or had an accident; or your children or spouse went on a spending spree—the guidelines provided herein will help you find freedom once more.

This book is presented in a simple format since its main goal is to lower your debt rather than teach economics (there *is*, however, one section for statistics inquirers). If time is money, this book has been designed to save you time in organizing and controlling your debt in a fast and efficient manner. The book can be approached in one of two ways:

THE APPROACH

- ✂ **From Beginning to End:** If you truly want to become more knowledgeable about your credit cards and learn how to control and lower your debt, read this book from beginning to end.
- ✂ **The Check Mark:** If you do not have the time to work through the entire book, but would like to know the most important methods for reducing your credit card debt, follow the check mark symbols (in the *table of contents*).

THE CHARACTERS

It is only reasonable to assume that there are many different types of consumers, each with different types of responsibilities and financial resources. With that thought in mind, the creation of several characters came about in *Credit Card Debt . . .* Suggested methods that might apply in different circumstances are represented throughout the book by using one or more of these unique characters.

Tom—the Student
A junior year college student. As a credit card issuer's favorite, he has received numerous credit card offers, yet he is fortunate enough to have accepted just two credit cards. He enjoys the freedom they give him, since he has little available cash and has always depended on his parents for income. Consequently, he has little knowledge of how to properly use and manage his credit cards. Currently, he carries a balance of $319.76 on just one card with an interest rate of 18.4%, and he pays only the monthly minimum.

Jennifer—the Extra Spender
A twenty-eight-year-old who recently started a career with an advertising company that pays her a comfortable salary. Lucky for her, Jennifer was able to avoid credit cards during her college years, mainly because students were not as heavily targeted then as they are now. However, because of her new monthly income and inexperience with credit cards, she's slowly digging a very deep hole with the ones she already has. At the moment she has $5,810.55 in debt, spread over three credit cards. The worst part about it is that she is paying an average interest rate of 18.72%.

Mr. and Mrs. Jones—the Next-Door Neighbors
A family with your average 2.3 children and a load of financial responsibilities. Mr. Jones is a computer consultant and Mrs. Jones works as a part-time nurse, so they are fortunate to have a constant flow of monthly income. They have already accumulated thousands of dollars in credit card debt with numerous credit cards. In addition, they used their credit cards to cover some recent unexpected expenses, raising their total credit card debt to $45,127.32, and since then have

been applying only minimum payments. The Joneses are unaware that the high average interest rate of 16.9% among their twelve credit cards and low minimum payment requirements are costing them hundreds of additional dollars each month.

Bob—the Should-Be Retiree

A fifty-nine-year-old divorced financial executive. Because of a disappointing investment decision, he has accumulated a large amount of credit card debt. He currently owes $20,933.97 on six credit cards at an overwhelming 17.35% average interest rate. Unfortunately, instead of saving for retirement, a substantial amount of his income is going toward his credit card debt. Because of the high interest, he is seeing very little of the debt declining, which worries him as he approaches retirement. Since he does not have much free time to take care of his personal finances, he is unable to effectively organize his debt and consequently lower its cost.

A Few Additional Comments Before Reading On

✂ There is no need for you to have any skills in accounting or finance. As long as you have a basic high school knowledge of math, you will be provided with all the information required for each step in the process.

✂ You will need a calculator. Everything else has been provided—except, for, of course, your credit cards. Please use pencils for the charts that have been provided; you will soon see why.

✂ Reducing your credit card debt works best with more than three credit cards. The more cards you have the better; you will need as much leverage as possible. If you are about to cancel any cards, please do not. If you

are offered any credit cards by mail, make sure to keep
the offers.

✂ Try to find a time in the day when you are the most
relaxed. Most credit card service representatives are
available twenty-four hours a day. Depending on the
number of credit cards you have, you might have to put
aside thirty minutes every five weeks or every five days
to manage your credit card debt.

✂ There is one important rule that must always be followed: You must always, with no exceptions, be organized. This is an essential key to conquering your debt.
If you are not organized, then you will ultimately not be
able to control your debt. Many credit card issuers
make their money from those who are not organized, as
you will see, so beware.

Let's move on!

Part One

The Road to Freedom

Step 1—Organizing

THE NEVER-ENDING STATEMENTS

You've probably already guessed that organization is the first major step in overcoming credit card debt. If you are well organized already, starting the process should not be hard. For those disorderly individuals, however, it is now time to follow a new path. Now, let's begin!

First, collect all your monthly statements from each of your credit cards, including past statements. You will want to separate all statements according to credit card, then arrange them by order of date. Put papers such as transfer checks, cash advance checks, and letters in separate piles.

It is recommended that you use a filing cabinet or a series of file folders. Each credit card should have its own file or section. Then make a separate file for all transfer checks and cash advance checks. Create a miscellaneous file for stray papers that do not belong anywhere specifically. Label everything. Once all that is in order, you'll need to be able to put these documents in a place where you'll have easy access to them.

You have now completed your first step in organization!

The next step will be to take all those important figures, such as current balance, interest rate, and credit limit, and place them onto one of several charts. If you've ever looked closely at some statements, they might seem to belong in another world. Be sure to take a look at the sample statement that has been provided on page 190, so that your statements become familiar and intelligible to you as we begin the process of organizing, analyzing, and reducing your debt.

Four charts are provided for your use; in them you will place important information about your credit cards. These charts are very important in managing your credit card debt. Make sure that all the information you are asked to provide is accurate and up-to-date.

- ✂ Chart #1—*"The Layout"*—offers vital information in keeping track of your credit cards, especially when planning balance transfers. It will be the most frequently used chart.
- ✂ Chart #2—*"The Details"*—provides specific information that is required when speaking to a customer service representative, traveling, or making payments.
- ✂ Chart #3—*"The Transfer"*— helps keep track of balances that are transferred between accounts.
- ✂ Chart #4—*"The Monthly Checkup"*—will help you organize and review your total balances and finance charges on a month-by-month basis.

THE CHARTS

No matter how many credit cards you have or how many balance transfers you need to make, whether your economic situation fits that of **Tom,** *or the* **Joneses,** *the following charts are essential in battling your credit card debt.*

THE LAYOUT

All individuals will greatly benefit from completing "The Layout" chart. It is essential to understanding and applying the recommendations of the book.

Take a look at "The Layout" chart at the end of this section; in it you will place vital, accurate, and up-to-date information. The information called for in the chart is essential to proceeding any further in the book, because it is the chart most frequently referred to throughout. Therefore, Tom needs to put down that term paper, Jennifer should resist from shopping tonight, the Joneses must put the children to bed, and Bob truly needs to postpone that trip to Florida.

It will be helpful to study the samples provided at the end of each section. Using Bob as an example, these charts reflect his credit card finances after he implemented the methods and recommendations found throughout the book. Blank charts have been provided at the end of each section for readers. So grab those charts, get comfortable, and let's get to work! (It is suggested that you make photocopies of all blank charts before writing down any data. And, when it is time to write, always use a pencil!)

✂ In the first column, "Credit Card," list your credit cards by name of issuer. List them in alphabetical order—in our example, we will use Bank One, Bank Two, Bank Three, and so on—and be consistent; use the same order in the other charts.

Credit Card
Bank One
Bank Two
Bank Three

✂ In the second column, "Balance," list your current outstanding balance; in other words, what you now owe to
  that particular credit card. This figure will change frequently, which is why it is recommended you use a pencil. Do not round off numbers; it is important to be
  exact. For example, if you owe $2,725.30, write
  $2,725.30.

Balance
$ 2,725.30
$ 4,250.65
$ 6,825.28

✂ In the third column, "Interest," write down whatever
  interest you are paying on that particular balance. The
  interest rate is otherwise known as the APR (annual
  percentage rate). Most likely there are different interest
  rates on your statement. These rates might apply to purchases, cash advances, and balance transfers. Once
  again, do not round off the numbers: If the rate is 8.9%,
  write down that figure. Sometimes more than one interest rate applies to your entire balance; for example, you
  might have transferred a balance at a special low interest rate to a credit card that already had a balance, but
  at a much higher interest rate. In such circumstances,
  write both rates down and specify what rate applies to
  which balance. You will then need to figure your average interest for the balances combined, a process later
  explained in *"What's Your Average?"* on page 48.

Interest
8.90%
16.95%
19.50%

✂ The fourth column, "Expires," relates to the expiration date of the interest rate in the "Interest" column. You need to know when that rate no longer applies to your balance. If your balance is linked with a special short-term low interest rate, chances are you will not be able to find the expiration date on your statement. Refer to the original letter that accompanied the offer or contact a customer service representative. This column is very important, for it will help you remember when you'll need to transfer your balance(s) or call customer service to make arrangements to extend the offer, which is explained throughout *"Step 3—Reducing,"* starting on page 53.

Expires
March 5/99
Variable
Variable

✂ The fifth column, "Limit," represents the actual credit limit you have on each credit card. This figure can easily be found on your statement and is useful to know, especially when you transfer balances. The higher your limit the better. In order to increase your credit limit you need to follow certain guidelines explained in "The Sky's the Limit," on page 96.

Limit
$ 2,800.00
$ 7,000.00
$ 7,500.00

✂ The sixth column, "Available," can be thought of as the "Limit" minus the "Balance." This figure will change every time your limit or balance changes. It shows how much credit you can still use, and again is important information as it relates to balance transfers.

Available
$ 74.70
$ 749.35
$ 674.72

✂ The seventh column, "Notes," will list anything of significant importance that needs to be noted, such as a fee for a balance transfer, an adjustment made by the customer service representative, an annual fee, and so on.

Notes
Balance—Cash Advance
Special 7.9% until April 99
Cash Advance Fee = 2%

You will notice that in Bob's chart there are totals for the "Balance," "Limit," and "Available" columns. He has also figured his average interest rate in the "Interest" column. It is a good idea to keep these figures up-to-date; plan to adjust them every four to five weeks. To figure the average interest rate for your balances, see "The Cost of Your Debt," on page 47. (Remember that the average interest rate [AIR] differs from annual percentage rate [APR] in that it represents the average of the APR and is used when two or more balances are involved in figuring the interest rate.)

On the left side of Bob's chart you will also notice the arrows linking the accounts. They will be used for planning balance transfers, which is further explained in "How to Plan Ahead," on page 69.

Overall, this explains the basics of "The Layout" chart. We now continue with our second chart, "The Details."

THE LAYOUT
(Sample)

	Credit Card	Balance	Interest	Expires	Limit	Available	Notes
1	Bank One	$2,725.30	8.90%	March 5/99	$2,800.00	$74.70	Balance—Cash Advance
2	Bank Two ②	$4,250.65	16.95%	Variable	$7,000.00	$749.35	Special 7.9% until April 99
3	Bank Three	$6,825.28	19.50%	Variable	$7,500.00	$674.72	Cash Advance Fee = 2%
4	Bank Four	$2,100.22	14.99%	February 99	$4,000.00	$1,899.78	Transfer by Phone Only
5	Bank Five ③	$1,134.63	17.90%	Variable	$8,000.00	$6,865.37	No Cash Advance Fee
6	Bank Six	$3,897.89	21%	Variable	$8,000.00	$102.11	Special 6.9% until May 99
7							
8							
9							
10		$20,933.97	17.35%		$37,300.00	$10,366.03	
		Total Debt	Avg. Inter.		Total Credit Limit	Total Available	

THE LAYOUT

Credit Card	Balance	Interest	Expires	Limit	Available	Notes
1	$	%		$	$	
2	$	%		$	$	
3	$	%		$	$	
4	$	%		$	$	
5	$	%		$	$	
6	$	%		$	$	
7	$	%		$	$	
8	$	%		$	$	
9	$	%		$	$	
10	$	%		$	$	
	Total Debt	Avg. Inter.		Total Credit Limit	Total Available	

THE DETAILS

Tom is the only individual who does not need to complete this chart since he has a relatively simple task of tracking only two credit cards. Jennifer will need it more in the future if she accumulates more credit cards but can get a head start now. The Joneses and Bob, however, will save time and much frustration in the long run by completing this chart now, since organization is most important when dealing with a large amount of debt and numerous credit cards.

"The Details" chart is where you will place a variety of specific information. This information will be useful when calling customer service, traveling, or in the event you lose your credit cards or statements, which seems to happen to the Joneses most frequently. Once again it is recommended that you follow Bob's sample chart at the end of this section. This will familiarize you with the following explanations before you fill out your own chart.

✂ In the first column: "Credit Card," simply list your credit cards as you did in "The Layout" chart.

Credit Card
Bank One
Bank Two
Bank Three

✂ In the second column, "Payee Name," fill in the name of the bank, or credit union, to which you would regularly write a check. You will be able to find this information on your statement. Do note that the payee name might be different if you plan to send a check without a payment stub and to a different address (see the section on the "Payment Address [without payment stub]" column later in this section). The Joneses have sometimes made payments to the wrong payee; even though their account is eventually credited, sometimes they have incurred additional finance charges and penalty fees. If you don't want the same experience the Joneses have had, make sure you know the correct payee(s) when sending payment without the payment stub.

Payee Name
Bank One
Bank Two
Bank Three

✂ The third column, "Account Type," is where you will list the type of credit card. For example: Credit Card One, Credit Card Two, or Credit Card Three.

Account Type
Credit Card One
Credit Card Two
Credit Card Three

✂ In the fourth column, "Account #," you will list the credit card's account number, which can always be found on the actual card or statement. Make sure the number is correct, since the account number is how companies track payments. It would be most unfortunate for you if someone else's account were to be credited for one of your payments.

Account #
2354-8740-2231-0000
2356-3366-3575-0000
5582-9598-8873-0000

✂ The fifth column, "Closing Date(s)," requires you to gather together your past statements. Closing dates are important; they tell you when your billing cycle regularly ends. Chances are that column will contain not just one date but a range. You need only look back about one year into your past statements; any further and you would be looking at dates that no longer truly reflect your current closing dates.

Closing Date(s)
15th–18th
11th
14th

✂ The sixth column, "Current Minimum," will note the minimum monthly amount that you have been required to pay. This figure, of course, will be decreasing as you pay off the credit card. You will want to see your latest statement for this information. This column will drastically change when you transfer balances. When updated, however, it will provide you with your total monthly obligations to your credit cards.

Current Minimum
$ 81.00
$ 85.00
$ 113.00

✂ In the seventh column, "Pay," is the amount that you are paying on a regular basis. If you are not paying a fixed amount every month you can ignore this column for now. Its importance is explained in further detail in "Minimum Payment—Tricks of the Trade," on page 85.

Pay
$ 85.00
$ 100.00
$ 170.00

✂ The eighth column, "Payment Address (without payment stub)," refers to the address to which you would have to send payment if you did not have the usual payment stub. For this information, you would need to contact a customer service representative. This is useful to know if you need to send a payment and you do not have access to the statement (for example, if you are traveling and your bank is making payments for you).

Payment Address (without payment stub)
Bank One, PO Box 8859, East Norwick, PA 11232
Bank Two, PO Box 5486, NY, NY 10012
Bank Three, PO Box 2356, Albany, NY 13409

✂ The ninth column, "Phone," is simple to understand. It is usually an 800 number that can be found on either your statement or the back of your credit card.

Phone
800-123-4567
800-859-7747
800-858-9875

✂ The tenth column, "International #," is important to have if you travel out of the United States. Toll-free 800 numbers do not usually work outside this country, so most credit cards have a number you can call collect when outside the country. Contact customer service at your credit card company for the number. (Some countries, such as Mexico, are setting up systems in which you can dial a U.S. 800 number. But to be safe, it is recommended that you find out the international number.)

International #
415-112-1243
212-556-5158
408-855-8695

✂ The eleventh column, "Monthly Minimum Configurations," deals mainly with how the credit card company determines your minimum payments. In order to find out the configurations, you will need to call customer service. It is convenient to have this information if you are ever without access to your statements.

Monthly Minimum Configurations
3% of balance
2% of balance
Divide balance by 60

✂ The twelfth column, "Notes," is to be used for whatever information you feel is important and does not apply to any of the previous columns.

Notes
$30.00 Annual Membership Fee
Limit was increased in March
No Membership Fee

"The Details" chart is very useful to those who wish to be very organized. Once you fill out all the information, there will no longer be a need to search for statements and credit cards when calling customer service, which will save you time and frustration. The chart is also especially useful when doing balance transfers on the phone, for many customer service reps will ask you for the account number, payee name, payment address, and so on at that time. And you'll be ready.

> *Ever wonder about those credit card registration services, the ones that claim to keep all your credit card information handy in the event you were to have your cards stolen or lost? Well, you'll never again have to consider subscribing to any such service, whether offered by your credit card issuer or an outside company. With "The Details" chart, your information will be accurate and organized. In the event your credit cards get lost or stolen, you will be prepared, and you'll save $20 or more a year—the fee generally charged for registering all your credit cards.*

After you take the time to fill in "The Details" chart, we then move on to "The Transfer" chart, a completely different type of chart that will make sure you keep track of your balance transfers between accounts.

THE DETAILS
(Sample)

	Credit Card	Payee Name	Account Type	Account #
1	Bank One	Bank One	Credit Card One	2354-8740-2231-0000
2	Bank Two	Bank Two	Credit Card Two	2356-3366-3575-0000
3	Bank Three	Bank Three	Credit Card Three	5582-9598-8873-0000
4	Bank Four	Bank Four	Credit Card Four	5428-9861-9567-0000
5	Bank Five	Bank Five	Credit Card Five	4325-9826-2292-0000
6	Bank Six	Bank Six	Credit Card Six	2349-3421-2567-0000
7				
8				
9				
10				

THE DETAILS
(Sample)

Closing Date(s)	Current Minimum	Pay	Payment Address (without payment stub)
15th–18th	$81.00	$85.00	Bank One, PO Box 8859, East Norwick, PA 11232
11th	$85.00	$100.00	Bank Two, PO Box 5486, NY, NY 10012
14th	$113.00	$170.00	Bank Three, PO Box 2356, Albany, NY 13409
3rd	$44.00	$60.00	Bank Four, PO Box 2222, NY, NY 10012
21st–22nd	$23.00	$40.00	Bank Five, PO Box 2356, Albany, NY 13409
6th	$72.00	$130.00	Bank Six, PO Box 3454, Miami, FL 12421

THE DETAILS
(Sample)

Phone	International #	Monthly Minimum Configurations	Notes
800-123-4567	415-112-1243	3% of balance	$30.00 Annual Membership Fee
800-859-7747	212-556-5158	2% of balance	Limit Was Increased in March
800-858-9875	408-855-8695	Divide balance by 60	No Membership Fee
800-987-5656	315-123-1234	Divide balance by 48	Cannot Call Collect
800-345-2211	215-989-3482	2% of balance	Limit Was Increased in October
800-989-3423	914-232-5422	Divide balance by 54	$55 Annual Membership Fee

THE DETAILS

Credit Card	Payee Name	Account Type	Account #
1			
2			
3			
4			
5			
6			
7			
8			
9			
10			

THE DETAILS

Closing Date(s)	Current Minimum	Pay	Payment Address (without payment stub)

THE DETAILS

Phone	International #	Monthly Minimum Configurations	Notes

THE TRANSFER

*Highly recommended for the **Joneses** and **Bob**, since they will most likely be doing a large number of balance transfers.*

"The Transfer" chart will help you keep track of transferring balances between credit cards. Every time you move a balance from one of your credit cards to another, you will need to place that information on this chart. It's a good idea to keep track of all your transfers, especially when handling more than one at a time.

Bob has made some transfers before and is familiar with the process. Unfortunately, he sometimes loses track and has made mistakes, which costs him more in finance charges. With "The Transfer" chart, he will have a record of where and when his transfers occurred.

The following is a list of the columns and their significance. Again, it is recommended that you follow Bob's example in the sample chart at the end of this section as you read on. Unless you have made some recent balance transfers, you will be filling in this chart later in the book.

✂ In the first column, "Transfer From," you will write the name of the credit card that is having its balance transferred.

Transfer From
Bank Six
Bank Six

✂ The second column, "Amount," is quite simply the amount of money that is being transferred. Remember to be exact.

Amount
$ 1,719.78
$ 2,048.11

✂ The third column, "Transfer To," is the final destination of the balance you are transferring; that is, a second credit card.

Transfer To
Bank Four
Bank Five

✂ In the fourth column, "Date," log the date in which either the transfer check was sent or the phone call (if using a customer service representative) was made.

Date
11/11/98
11/11/98

✂ In the fifth column, "Completed," is the actual date the transfer was posted. Check your statement. Chances are it will take a few weeks after your check was sent or you called. In this instance, be forewarned not to stop making payments to the account in question. If, for example, you are planning to transfer the full amount from an account, it is suggested that you instead transfer that amount *less* the next minimum payment, especially if payment is due in a week or so (if the remaining balance is \$2,176.38 and the minimum due is \$45.00, pay \$45.00 and transfer the remaining \$2,131.38.

Completed
11/19/98
11/20/98

✂ The sixth column, "Notes," provides another opportunity for you to make useful notes not covered elsewhere.

Notes
Done over the Phone
Sent Check

You will find that "The Transfer" chart is essential if you are making numerous balance transfers. By keeping this record you will save time and effort in accounting for your transactions.

If you take a look at Bob's "The Transfer" chart you will see that not all of the transfers equal the original credit card balance being transferred, because he would also make regular monthly payments—apart from transferring balances—to his creditors. The importance of this is explained in detail in "Minimum Payment—Tricks of the Trade," on page 85.

If you are unfamiliar with transferring balances, it is strongly suggested that you read through "Step 3—Reducing," beginning on page 53, before filling out any information. This section explains the essential methods to use, and traps to avoid, when transferring balances.

The next section leads us to the final chart, "The Monthly Checkup," a simple, yet enjoyable chart to use.

THE TRANSFER
(Sample)

	Transfer From	Amount	Transfer To	Date	Completed	Notes
1	Bank Six	$1,719.78	Bank Four	11/11/98	11/19/98	Done over the Phone
2	Bank Six	$2,048.11	Bank Five	11/11/98	11/20/98	Sent Check
3	Bank Two	$4,150.65	Bank Six	11/20/98	12/2/98	Sent Check
4	Bank Five	$3,182.74	Bank Six	11/30/98	12/10/98	Sent Check
5	Bank Three	$6,655.28	Bank Two	12/5/98	12/17/98	Done over the Phone

THE TRANSFER

	Transfer From	Amount	Transfer To	Date	Completed	Notes
1						
2						
3						
4						
5						
6						
7						
8						
9						
10						

THE MONTHLY CHECKUP

*This chart is vital to **all individuals**. It is important to see how one is doing on a month-to-month basis.*

It is a good idea to keep track of your balances and finance charges on a month-to-month basis. Not only will "The Monthly Checkup" chart help you know where you stand, but, psychologically, it will please you when you see your balances and finance charges decreasing every month. In Jennifer's case, this will help organize and visualize her credit card debt and at the same time make her realize what her spending is really costing her.

✂ The first column, "Date," is the place to keep track of the date on which the balances and finance charges were added to the chart. It is very important that this date remain consistent. If you update your accounts on the twenty-third of the month, continue in each successive month to do so. It is best to choose a date *after* you receive the last statement of the month.

Date
Sept. 98
Oct. 98

✂ In the second column, "Balance Total," you will place your total current balance from all your credit cards. As long as you keep "The Layout" chart up-to-date, this should be easy.

Balance Total
$ 20,933.97
$ 20,651.64

✂ In the third column, "Finance Total," add the finance charges from each of your credit cards and place the grand total in this column. Rather than retrieving the figure from each statement each month, you might make a note of each on a separate sheet as you receive them, or in the "Notes" column of "The Layout" chart. In the end, it will save you time.

Finance Total
$ 302.67
$ 283.96

✂ The numbered columns, "1" through "10," will be used in tracking your credit card statements. The numbers will correspond with the credit cards listed in "The Layout" chart. It is a good idea to keep track of your billing statements, simply because there are times when the postal system is not perfect—and it would be unfortunate to be charged a late fee or get a negative mark on your credit report for a billing statement you never received. Just check off each box when a statement has been paid and sent. It will also be pleasing to see that as your balance decreases so does the number of credit card statements that must be paid.

1	2	3	4	5	6	7	8	9	10
x	x	x	x	x	x				
x	x	x	x	x	x				

This chart will be the most fun to watch over time. By following the rules in the later sections, you will see your debt decrease at a very fast rate. Once you've succeeded in manipulating lower interest rates for all your credit cards, take a look back at the first total finance charge and you'll be amazed at how much you are saving. (And how much you were being robbed!) If you choose to maintain your records on a computer, it is recommended that you use a spreadsheet program in place of the charts and a financial management software program such as Quicken to help keep track of your credit cards, payments, and balance transfers.

Pretty simple? I hope it was not too much work. Just remember that by being organized and noticing every detail of your credit card debt you become more powerful, and the credit card issuers become *less* powerful in being able to take advantage of you!

We are now ready to move ahead to "Step 2—Analyzing," which can begin only when "The Layout" chart has been completed, so make sure you have finished all necessary columns in the chart before leaving this section.

THE MONTHLY CHECKUP
(Sample)

	Date	Balance Total	Finance Total	1	2	3	4	5	6	7	8	9	10
1	Sept. 98	$20,933.97	$302.67	x	x	x	x	x	x				
2	Oct. 98	$20,651.64	$283.36	x	x	x	x	x	x				
3	Nov. 98	$20,350.00	$220.45	x	x	x	x	x	x				
4	Dec. 98	$19,985.46	$166.55	x	x	x	x	x					
5	Jan. 99	$19,567.01	$105.98	x	x	x	x	x					
6	Feb. 99	$19,087.99	$103.39	x	x	x	x	x					
7	March 99	$18,606.38	$100.78	x	x	x	x	x					
8	April 99	$18,122.16	$98.16	x	x	x	x	x					
9	May 99	$17,635.32	$95.52	x	x	x	x						
10	June 99	$17,145.84	$92.87	x	x	x	x						
11	July 99	$16,653.71	$90.21	x	x	x							
12	Aug. 99	$16,158.92	$87.53	x	x	x							

Less Credit Card Debt: $(4,775.05)

Total Interest Paid: $1,747.47

THE MONTHLY CHECKUP

Date	Balance Total	Finance Total	1	2	3	4	5	6	7	8	9	10
1												
2												
3												
4												
5												
6												
7												
8												
9												
10												
11												
12												
Totals:	$	$										

Step 2—Analyzing

YOUR FLEXIBILITY

*Determining your flexibility is important for those who have accumulated a significant amount of debt. This would include the **Joneses** and **Bob**. It's not as important for **Tom** and **Jennifer**, though, since they have not accumulated a large amount of credit card debt.*

Now for the fun part: seeing where you can save money! Unfortunately, you had to do a little work to get here, but it's well worth the amount of money you will start to save.

The first question you need to ask yourself is: How much credit card debt do I have? To find the answer, just add all the balances in "The Balance" column of "The Layout" chart. It helps to keep this total written below all the balances (just as in the sample) and to update it frequently. Follow by asking yourself: What is my total credit limit? Simply add all the limits from that column. The larger the difference between your total debt and your total credit limit, the more flexibility you will have. It is ideal for your total debt to be no more than 50% of your total limit. If you are above this figure, you will be less flexible. Conversely, if you are below this figure, you will have more flexibility with your credit cards.

A good way to determine your flexibility is to divide your

total limit by your total balance. Any number above 2 means that you have very good flexibility, and any number below 2 means a less advantageous flexibility.

THE FORMULA

Total Limit / Total Balance = Flexibility Rating

High Flexibility

$32,000.00 / $14,112.98 = 2.27

Low Flexibility

$32,000.00 / $25,133.77 = 1.27

In relation to credit cards, think of flexibility as the ability to move balances and thereby receive lower interest rate offers. The higher your flexibility rating, the more money you will be able to save. Try to remember that it is important to be flexible and that your struggle with credit cards will depend on it. But even if you have a low flexibility rating, you will be able to increase your flexibility by following the methods in this book. Generally speaking, decreasing one's debt, lowering interest rates, increasing credit limits, or being approved by a new credit card will help increase your flexibility rating. So even after the Joneses discover that their flexibility rating is a low 1.08, they should not worry, for there is still hope of increasing it.

It is recommended that every few months you check your flexibility rating, since it should be increasing. If it is decreasing, you should investigate why. It might mean an increase in your total balance or a decrease in available credit limits—or both.

You now know how flexible your credit card debt is, but

do you know how much it is truly costing you? We move to the next section, "The Cost of Your Debt," to find the answer.

THE COST OF YOUR DEBT

*This is important for **all individuals**, since everyone needs to know the realistic cost of maintaining their debt. If you have only one credit card, it's easy to figure out!*

Now that you know how deep a hole you're in and how much you can move within that hole, it's time to see how much deeper it is going with those interest rates. You might be relieved to know that the average American consumer pays around 17% in interest on credit cards. Whether this is because these consumers have no money and are accessing cash advances, they aren't aware of the interest they are paying, or they just don't care is anyone's guess. What is known is that there are consumers who are paying higher interest rates and consumers who are paying lower rates. My goal is to get *you* to pay less, much less!

Lets start with the AIR, or average interest rate.

Tom, Jennifer, the Joneses, and Bob will now begin to realize the true reason their credit card debt fails to reduce significantly each month and why the credit card business is the most profitable type of bank loan.

You are probably wondering where you stand in terms of your AIR, or, perhaps, how much those credit cards are really getting from you. Take a look at the following example, using Jennifer's credit card debt figures.

WHAT'S YOUR AVERAGE?

1. In Jennifer's case, she took the balance on a credit card and multiplied it by the interest that applied. This gave her the interest she would pay in one year.

$2,498.64 x .195* = $487.23

   She did this for each credit card.

2. Then she added all the interest that would be applied to each credit card in one year.

$487.23   + $427.94   + $172.83 = $1,088.00
Card 1   Card 2   Card 3   Total Interest

3. Then all the balances were added (this should have already been done on "The Layout" chart).

$2.498.64   + $2,324.33   + $987.58 = $5,810.55
Card 1   Card 2   Card 3   Total Balance

4. Then she divided the total interest amount (Step 2) by the total of all balances (Step 3).

$1,088.00 / $5,810.55 = .1872
Total Interest / Total Balance = Average Interest Rate

5. Finally, Jennifer ended up with the average interest rate she was paying toward all her combined credit cards.

18.72% = Average Interest Rate**

---

*Remember to move the decimal point two places to the left when working with interest rates. So an interest rate of 19.5% becomes .195.

**Certain factors such as the grace period and the way the credit card issuer

So now you know where you stand. By seeing that Jennifer is paying an 18.72% average interest rate, we can come to the conclusion that she can significantly reduce the cost of her credit card debt by at least 60% or more. So let's get those credit cards and attack the ones with the highest interest rates first, since they are what's causing your high AIR. We'll begin in the next section, "Categorize Your Credit Cards."

CATEGORIZE YOUR CREDIT CARDS

*The more credit cards you have, the more important it is to read this section. Therefore, the **Joneses** and **Bob** should read on. Even though **Tom** and **Jennifer** do not have numerous credit cards, it is important to know which ones should be dealt with first.*

The Joneses and Bob face a common problem: too many credit cards that are not properly managed. It is important for them to find out not only the cost of their debt but also which credit cards are the most costly to them.

You can think of this process as a type of police lineup in which you will see who is robbing you the most. If there is more than one victimizer, we will find out here and now.

First, let's take a look at your "Interest" column in "The Layout" chart. How does it look? You can take a quick glance and see how many double digits and single digits you have in interest rates. If they are all double digits (anything above 10%), then you are paying too much. Though there might be just a few, they still must be eliminated.

---

determines the finance charge might offset one's average interest rate. However, the average interest rate as calculated here will be close to accurate. The section entitled "Interest, Interest, and Interest," on page 101, will explain the other complications involved in determining the finance charge.

Now take a closer look. A 9.9% rate can be thought of as 10%. Many credit card issuers offer rates that end in .9 to make them more attractive, which is just like the 99 cents theory of making a product look cheaper than it really is. You'll also want to take a look at when those single rates expire, because when they do, the interest will surely rise into the double digits.

You need to separate the interest rates into three categories: high, medium, and low (you can categorize them any way you like—bad, badder, and baddest, for example), as long as you remember the order.

LINE 'EM UP

✂ "High interest rates" should be considered any interest rate above 15%.

✂ "Medium interest rates" should be considered any interest rate between 14.99% and 9.5%.

✂ "Low interest rates" are anything below 9.49%.

Now that you have separated the rates into three groups, you have also separated the credit cards. You now know which are priority and which don't need immediate attention. One useful technique in separating the three groups is to use highlighters. Select three colors and highlight each credit card according to its category of high, medium, or low interest rate. You can use "The Layout" chart and highlight the names under the "Credit Card" column, or use an additional piece of paper. Just take a look at the following sample using Bob's figures from his "The Layout" chart.

Credit Card	Balance	Interest	Category
1. Bank One	$ 2,725.30	8.90%	Low
2. Bank Two	$ 4,250.65	16.95%	High
3. Bank Three	$ 6,825.28	19.50%	High
4. Bank Four	$ 2,100.22	14.99%	Medium
5. Bank Five	$ 1,134.63	17.90%	High
6. Bank Six	$ 3,897.89	21.00%	High

Now that you have organized your credit cards by interest rates, we move on.

Let's first look at the high interest rate credit cards. Do any of these cards have expiring rates? You might be surprised to discover that a 15.6% rate can be a special introductory offer that will soon rise as high as 22%. Chances are most of the highest rates are *not* special offers, but if any are, they're the first to attack. If you take a look at Bob's *"The Transfer"* chart on page 37, the first balance he deals with is from his Bank Six card with an interest rate of 21%, the highest of all his credit cards.

It has been recommended by others that you should focus first on a credit card with the smallest *balance*, even if it doesn't apply the highest interest. The thought here is that, psychologically, it would be more effective in the end to get one credit card completely out of your way. I disagree. As long as you can control your emotions, you will begin to save money by concentrating on the highest interest rate card (or cards) first.

Once you're done organizing and lowering your high rate cards, you will move down to cards with the lower interest rates. Remember, just because a card has a lower rate now doesn't necessarily mean it will stay there; in a month it could be back in the *higher interest rate* category, so always stay on your toes!

(Techniques to maintain continuous low interest rates are explained throughout the book. There are several ways to approach lowering your interest rates: wait for special mail and telephone offers, call customer service representatives and ask what they are offering, or call customer service representatives using the Words of Power and have them offer you a special interest rate! These methods are explained in the next section, "Step 3—Reducing.")

Now that you have organized your credit card debt and determined which cards must be dealt with first, it is time to move on. You are no longer a casualty in the war against credit card debt. With all the preparation this book has provided so far you are now armed and ready, and it is now time to go into the field and engage in battle!

Step 3—Reducing

NOW FOR THE FUN PART

*An important aspect that separates **Tom** and **Jennifer** from the **Joneses** and **Bob** is free time and a lack of financial responsibilities. Unfortunately, these don't usually come together. The Joneses and Bob might find it difficult to put aside time to manage their credit card debt, but if they are able to put aside a few minutes each week it will go a long way toward saving them a significant amount of money.*

You probably now know more about your credit card debt than ever before. In the following sections you will learn even more: what credit card companies will never tell you. Remember, they'd like you to stay in debt as *long* as possible (as long as you make your monthly payments), while you'd like to get out of debt as *soon* as possible. These are two conflicting sides in a battle that seems never-ending. You need to take control of your debt, and credit card issuers make it hard. You need to know how much you are paying in interest, what's going toward your balance, what fees you have paid and why, and so on. Do you think credit card issuers are going to send you letters stating how much you paid in interest for the year and giving your total payments for late fees and cash advances? They would lose a lot of customers if they did. If they don't have to tell you, chances are they won't. It is quite easy to think that you paid, perhaps, only $30 in finance charges last month, but multiply that by twelve and you get $360 of interest for one card in one year. That is enough to buy a round-trip ticket to Mexico!

When you call a customer service representative, they can see right away whether you have paid on time, what your balance is, how many times you have had late payments, and so on. You need to be just as prepared or you will be at a great disadvantage. With the charts and suggestions from this book, you will be.

Let's consider the many ways to reduce your credit card debt.

✂ The first option is to wait for special offers in the mail, which is somewhat like waiting for the enemy to make the first move. (Accepting those pre-approved credit card offers is probably how many of us got caught with credit card debt in the first place. But now you will learn how to use those offers to your advantage.)

✂ The second option is to call credit card issuers and see if they are offering any special interest rates. You might be surprised by the results of just asking. In this situation, you are making the first move.

✂ The third option is to call credit card issuers and tell them why they should give you a lower rate. You might be surprised at how they will respond. Not only are you making the first move, but it's an aggressive and positive one.

Do not skip these methods; follow them in order. You would feel silly following the third option and making an aggressive move when you have already received a low interest rate offer by mail. We will now go into a more detailed explanation of these three options.

PRE-APPROVED?

Have you ever been rejected by a pre-approved credit card offer and wondered why? In fact, this is a very misleading statement. The fact of the matter is, you have merely been screened. It is a marketing scheme that actually works. Those who think they've been approved submit to filling out a form, which provides the credit card issuers with information that is used to decide whether an individual is really *pre-approved. Credit card issuers claim this is just because they do actually approve of certain categories of individuals— college students, for example.*

OFFERS BY MAIL AND PHONE

*Every type of individual is subject to credit card offers. Credit card issuers market toward all types for various reasons. However, individuals such as **Tom** will most likely receive more offers and approvals than the **Joneses**, who are already burdened by credit cards.*

Credit card issuers love individuals like Tom. With little or no financial responsibilities, support from parents, exaggerated spending habits, and lack of understanding of personal finances, these people prove to be some of the most profitable customers for credit card issuers. Although some universities shun the idea of abusing students, others have taken on the motto "If you can't beat them, join them." They do this by allowing banks and credit unions to promote their credit cards by using the university name. (See *"The College Students,"* on page 122.)

Whether it is a new credit card or a credit card you

already own that is offering a special interest rate, both have one thing in common: the desire to bait you into becoming or remaining a customer and to eventually ensnare you with a very high interest rate (usually two to three times larger than the original low rate). Most commonly offered are checks issued to you at a very low interest rate. These low rates are otherwise known as "teaser rates."

Teaser rates are designed to trick you by offering a low interest rate for a short period of time, usually between three and nine months, before jumping to a much higher interest rate. But if you stay organized and know when these rates are going to expire, you are the one who will be teasing the credit cards! Such offers are common from credit cards you already own, especially when you have had a large balance in the past and now have a low or zero balance. You will notice this pattern as you start to transfer many balances: The more transfers you make, the more teaser rates you will be offered. Eventually you will have your hands filled with various teaser rate offers. You can use most of these special checks for purchases, cash advances, or transfers. If you want to get out of debt, do not use them for purchases. How can you get out of debt if you keep buying presents? Cash advances should only be used wisely (explained in "Cash Advance—Friend or Foe?" on page 104). The only valuable use for these checks is to transfer balances, which is explained throughout the rest of Step 3.

Credit card issuers are no longer using only our postal system, they're also having customer representatives call you at your home. This helps increase their market share at a relatively low cost. When you receive phone calls, do not think right away that someone is trying to sell you some silly product; it might just be the credit card issuer offering you a special balance transfer rate. Even though some will send you checks, many will process your transaction only over the phone. So if you are unprepared, ask if you can call back later so you can organize your statements before making transfers. Just make sure they make a note of the special interest offer to your account, since you don't want to end up calling back to learn that the only offer available is a high 17.99%!

Special rate checks received by mail or offered over the phone can really help you save money and even build morale in your struggle against credit card debt. The more special rate checks you have, the more flexible you will be with your debt. Before you know it, you will be transferring balances with 7.9% interest rates to other accounts for 5.9% interest rates or less.

The Joneses are often overwhelmed with credit card offers and teaser rates from credit cards they already own. Since they usually have relatively little time to review the offers, they put them aside until later in the week, when they can take a further look at what is being offered. So before you use one of these checks, or make transfers over the phone, make sure the offer is worthwhile, as do the Joneses.

Every time you plan a balance transfer you will need to review the following questions.

REVIEW THE DETAILS

- ✂ What is the interest rate and for how long?
- ✂ How much available credit do you have on the credit card that is offering the checks?
- ✂ Are there any additional charges, such as a cash advance fee, for using the checks?*

---

*Some credit card issuers apply cash advance rules to transfers, such as not offering a 30-day grace period on the transfer. What that means is that as soon as the transfer is made, it will incur interest. Also note that some credit cards will not apply the finance charge on the first statement; it might not

✂ Are there any balances that you are paying a higher interest rate toward, and if so, is there enough available credit from the special offer to cover those balances?

✂ Is there already a balance on the credit card that is offering the special checks? If so, what is the interest rate?

So it seems all you have to do is get the special low-rate checks, make sure they have not yet expired, and transfer your balance, right? Well, it's not as simple as it sounds. There are certain situations you need to be aware of. Continue to read on, because you are about to learn the sleazy tricks credit cards have up their magnetic strips.

PAYING TWO RATES FOR ONE BALANCE?

An important question asked in the last section ("Review the Details") was: Is there already a balance on the credit card that is offering the special checks? If so, what is the interest rate? In other words, if you are planning to make a transfer to an account that already has a balance, you might be caught with higher interest rates. Why? Because you will now have two different rates on one balance with one credit card. Sound confusing? Read on, and you will find out how so many credit card consumers are caught by this credit card trap.

Every credit card issuer has a different system of payment distribution, otherwise known as "application of payments." In the case of balance transfers, some companies will have a certain percentage of your payment apply to a lower rate and

---

appear until the statement following the period in which you pay off, or transfer, your balance once again. So don't be surprised when a fee is due even though you thought you paid off everything. Some credit card issuers, however, might treat the transfer under the same terms as a regular purchase, which is much more preferable and saves the consumer a lot of complications, such as those explained in "How to Plan Ahead," on page 69.

the remaining percentage apply to the higher rate—for example, 25% of your payment might go to the balance with the lower rate while the other 75% goes to the balance with the higher rate. Some credit card companies might even attempt to apply your entire payment to the balance with the higher rate.*

Now is the time to ask questions, because here is where they can really catch you!

For example, let's say you do a six-month transfer of $2,500 at a special rate of 5.9% from a credit card company with which you already have a balance of $3,500 at 15.9%. You now have two different rates for two different balances, and soon find that only a small portion, or no portion, of your actual monthly payment is being made toward the lower interest rate balance. You've probably thought that it makes sense to pay off the higher balance in the first place. Generally, that is true, but in this case it is not. If you are making large payments to the credit card and plan to have the whole balance paid off before six months, then you will be fine. However, if you are only paying the minimum due or slightly more, and you plan to do so for more than six months, chances are you will find yourself in trouble, because the balance with the lower rate will suddenly jump very high, most likely higher than the original 15.9%.

Before Six Months

5.9% = Special Balance Transfer Offer,
15.9% = Purchases,
19% = Cash Advances

---

*Some credit card issuers might apply your payment only to the balance that is under the promotional rate. In turn, the remaining balance increases daily, with a high interest rate, with no payments crediting the balance. This is a great way for the credit card issuers to benefit from compounding interest.

After Six Months

15.9% = Purchases,
19% = Cash Advances (Expired 5.9% Balance Offer)

The larger portion of your payments (if not all of them) will now apply to the original 15.9%, and the most recent balance, which was at 5.9%, is now accumulating interest at a rate of 19% (over three times the original interest). Your plan has backfired! Any payment made to the balance with the 19% will most likely barely cover the interest applied to that balance. In the end, you'll be saddled with a balance that will appear to be consistent every month! (And you'll notice that you've just been strategically attacked by your credit card.)

So how do you pay off the balance at the higher interest rate? After first paying the balance at 15.9%, the remaining portion of your payments will apply to the 19% balance. By then, you will probably have accumulated a lot of finance charges, so what about calling customer service and asking that your payments go toward the higher rate balance? Chances are they will not change the rules, for that is precisely how they make their money, and they will do so as long as it is legal. Keep in mind that if there is an opportunity for credit card issuers to make more money, they will not hesitate!*

So you are now aware of the tricks up the sleeves of the credit card issuers. Even with all your careful planning, you've found yourself locked into a balance with a high interest rate that is increasingly hard to pay off. Let's see

---

*This section actually applies not only to transferred balances but also to purchases and cash advances. The same situation as described above would also occur once the individual with an outstanding balance either makes a purchase or takes a cash advance on the same credit card through a special low-rate offer.

what you might have done to prevent this situation when you receive a special offer and you already have a balance in your account. The first thing to do is estimate the average interest rate if you were to make a balance transfer.

Take a look at the following example of how the Joneses were able to figure their average interest rate before accepting an offer, using the same figures and circumstances previously explained.

Numbers Don't Lie!

1. $3,500 × 15.9% / 2* = $278.25   Original Balance
2. $2,500 × 5.9% / 2* = $73.75   Transferred Balance
3. $278.25 + $73.75 = $352.00   Interest in Six Months
4. $352.00 / $6,000 × 2** = 11.73%   Average Interest Rate†

We can see that, following the transfer, the actual interest rate between the two balances would be 11.73% for the Joneses. The original special offer of 5.9% definitely does not look as appealing as it first did, but they will not give up so easily. After studying these numbers, it is easy to see why a credit card would offer such an interest rate: It is very profitable! Although most consumers initially see the rate as 5.9%, the credit card issuers see it as 11.73%. If the consumers saw the 11.73% interest rate to begin with, they would probably think twice before transferring any balance.

The next example represents the credit card issuer's profit over six months resulting from finance charges. The

---

*Dividing by 2 represents half of a year, or six months.

**Multiplying by 2 is used to determine interest for one year

†To keep the example simple and straightforward payments and/or transaction fees have not been included in determining the average interest rate.

figures demonstrate that even though the interest rate is lower, the balance has increased, which in turn will provide a larger profit to the credit card issuer.*

From the Creditor's Viewpoint

$3,500 × 15.9% / 2 = $278.25 Original Balance

$6,000 × 11.73% /2 = $351.90 Both Balances

This section has illustrated how profitable it can be for the credit card issuer to offer the six-month low interest rate package but not how that rate will benefit the consumer.

So is it *ever* cost-effective to accept a special low interest rate offer? Once you're able to pay both balances at a 5.9% interest rate, it certainly is. In the next section, you will learn how to use the lower interest rate to its fullest advantage, a maneuver bringing you one step closer to winning the credit card war.

PAY ONE RATE FOR ONE BALANCE!

So how does one manage to lock in both balances at a 5.9% interest rate? To begin with, you want to ask yourself the general questions that were listed under "Review the Details," on page 57. Most important, you do not want to make a transfer to an account that already has a balance with a much higher rate. What you want to do is first clear that balance you will have the full credit limit available at 5.9% when the lower rate is offered.

If we keep using our previous sample figures, the first

---

*A difference of $73.65 between the combined and the original balances might not seem like much. Imagine, however, that there are 40,000 card members in a similar situation. The six-month total would nearly be an additional $3 million.

question you'll most likely ask yourself is: How can I possibly pay off $3,500? You won't have to, but you will be able to put it out of your way temporarily by transferring it to another credit card. When the transfer is complete, you can transfer the same $3,500 back to the original credit card at a rate of 5.9%, no longer paying the 15.9% rate. (You can also leave it where it was transferred, as long as that interest rate is considerably low.)

If this sounds confusing, just take a look at Bob's "The Transfer" chart, on page 37, in which he transferred his Bank Six balance with an interest of 21% to two other credit cards. He was then able to fully utilize the 6.9% special interest rate offer on his Bank Six card (as noted in the "Notes" column of his "The Layout" chart on page 18) for the full $8,000 limit. This is one good reason you should never throw out transfer checks, at least not until they expire.

But what happens if you do not have enough credit available from another credit card to make the transfer? The first step is to find out how much you can transfer. If it's only $2,000, ask yourself if there is another credit card to which you might transfer the remaining $1,500. Keep in mind that other credit card issuers will be more than happy to have your transfer in their account as long as you abide by their rules. That means, of course, that you do not exceed your available credit limit and that you pay any additional fees that might apply to the transfer. Fees are generally 2% of the balance, while others may be a flat fee, i.e., $20. (There *are* a few credit cards that do charge a higher fee.) When you can think how much you will be able to save with a 5.9% interest rate, 2% certainly is not much. And sometimes there might not even be a transaction fee, which is always a plus!*

---

*Transaction fees are sometimes negotiable, and often are waived for balance transfers done over the phone. Remember, it doesn't hurt to ask!

When transferring the $3,500 to another credit card, it is advisable to choose a card with the lowest rate possible. But don't despair if the other credit card has a similar high interest rate, because you will be using that card only for a week or so. If the transaction is considered a cash advance, you will end up paying interest for the week, or for the number of days the balance was in the account. But once again, it will be well worth the effort when you receive a 5.9% interest rate, especially if it is for at least six months or more. Also note that some credit cards will increase your credit limit at the time of a balance transfer if you simply ask. Don't expect a huge credit increase; several hundred dollars rather than several thousand is usual. (For further information on increasing your credit limit, see "The Sky's the Limit," on page 96.) The final question, then, is how much will you save by going through all this trouble?

For the answer, we return to the Joneses, who are able to use the full potential of the 5.9% interest rate offer. See the chart below.

Savings Over Twelve Months

1. $3,500 × .159 = $556.50 15.9% Interest
2. $3,500 × .059 = $206.50 5.9% Interest
3. $556.50 − $206.50 = $350.00   Savings

In the equations above, we can see that the Joneses save the $350 difference between the 15.9% and the 5.9% interest rates (minus any transaction fees) after spending just a few minutes of their time. They can now transfer the remaining $2,500 for the same 5.9% interest rate without paying an average interest rate of 11.73%, saving even more.

When you begin, the task of comparing and transferring

balances might seem time-consuming and complicated, but as your skills sharpen it becomes much simpler.

At this point, you might be thinking that it is unfair to compare the two rates, since the higher rate of 15.9% is the standard rate for the account and the lower 5.9% is offered for only six months. Though that is true, there are ways to extend the special low rate offer, and we'll soon find out how.

> A Word of Advice: *If you are transferring a balance and you have the option of choosing one of two credit cards with a low 5.9% interest rate and no transaction fees, choose the one that offers the 5.9% for the longer amount of time. If they are equal, choose the one with the largest credit limit.*

Remember that credit card issuers know that consumers "surf" for better rates or use their low interest rates to their best advantage. Although there is little the companies can do to stop the surfing, something they have done is impose time limits on the offers, usually three to five weeks. But that is usually more than enough time to complete the transactions, so there's no need for concern. (For more detailed information on properly timing the transfers, see "You Have Until Dawn," on page 68.) Another battle has just been won by the consumer. But read on as another one is waged!

Special Holiday Checks ... Beware!

After receiving and accepting a low transfer balance rate, it is not unusual to find that the same credit card issuer is offering another interest rate for balance transfers several weeks later. That offer will claim a special low interest rate for balance transfers; however, it will usually not claim the exact interest rate it is offering, but more likely state something such as: "Transfer balances from other cards that charge up to 21% or more interest," while at the same time offering a "30-day grace period that will save you lots of money!"

Sometimes these offers do not mention any interest rate at all, but instead recommend using special checks to make Christmas shopping easier. You might think it's a great offer at first, or perhaps a continuation of a previous offer that has expired, but soon you'll wonder why, if you're being offered such a special low interest rate, it isn't being advertised. You might find that the answer is because the attached interest rates are 18% or 19%—and sometimes even higher. This can be costly to those who confuse their previous special balance transfer rates with new rates attached to the additional checks. In Jennifer's case, she ended up making several purchases with the checks, unaware that they were tied to an astonishing 19.8% interest rate.

If you already have a balance at a low rate, such as the 5.9% previously mentioned, and you use one of these special checks at an unknown interest rate, you'll end up paying a higher average interest rate on the combined balances. The credit card issuer would then have you back in the same situation we just encountered in "Paying Two Rates for One Balance?" The solution to the problem is simple. When you receive a new offer, call customer service and find out the exact interest rate and whether there are any transaction fees. Not everything that glitters is gold!

NO INTEREST?

Nothing is free in this world, and credit cards are no exception. Whether they are motivated by competition or by a thirst for making more money, credit card issuers are doing whatever they can to attract new customers and maintain existing ones. Unfortunately, many customers are finding out the hard way that most of the low interest rate offers usually have hidden costs. These costs are the backbones of profit for credit card issuers.

Take, for example, an offered 0% interest rate for four months. Probably sounds very good at first. In fact, it would probably get your immediate attention. But in terms of transferring balances, such offers can have very high hidden costs. For example, the 0% interest rate checks might be applied as cash advances, and in the fine print, all that might be noted is: "These checks are applied as a cash advance to be repaid under the terms and conditions of account." Not very specific, for which there is probably a reason. Again, you will need to call customer service for the exact details and transaction fees, if any.

Tom thought he was getting a great deal. He grabbed "The Details" chart to have all the required information handy to take advantage of this unbelievable offer. He called customer service and was prepared to do the transfer over the phone. Finally, just before authorizing the transaction, he asked if there were any transaction fees. The representative mentioned that there was a transaction fee of 4%. At first it didn't seem like much, but Tom wanted to do the math and said he would call back later.

He figured that since the 0% was for only four months, the 4% transaction fee was like paying 1% of the balance each month, the same as if the balance was under an interest rate of 12% (1% × 12 months = 12%). So he concluded that the 0% interest rate was just another credit card advertisement hoax. Tom, of course, never called back.

When such offers like the 0% interest rate end, the interest could jump as high as 18% or 20%. If you are unprepared for the increase, you might end up paying quite a bit in finance charges on that 0% offer, which was originally supposed to save you money. Chances are, you'll probably look back at that interest rate with much less amazement than before. So always check, double-check, and never make any transfers of balances unless you know for sure if there are hidden costs. Remember, if you are unsure of an offer, confirm it with the issuer—if it sounds too good to be true, it usually is!

YOU HAVE UNTIL DAWN

Or close to it, since there is always a time limit when transferring balances. Most of the special low interest rate offers have cutoff dates. For example, if the checks expire June 10, that means they must be posted to the account before that date. If you do not plan ahead, you could end up paying higher interest rates.

If you were to miss the cutoff date, your checks might still be valid but tied to the regular—not the special—interest rate for that account. If for some reason, however, the amount posted to your account exceeds the cutoff date by only a few days, the credit card issuer might still allow access to the low interest rate. If not, you should call the customer service department, which might be able to remedy the situation for you.

Remember that the due dates are usually within three to five weeks from the time you receive the offer. However, some due dates can be as short as ten days, while others might be as long as the interest rate is valid, which can mean several months to a year. When you receive an offer with a very low interest rate, make sure to make a note of it in your "The Layout" chart. The last thing you want is to pull out those checks with the 4.9% rate and find out that they expired the previous week. When you receive additional offers from other credit cards that you do not wish to make any transfers into, hold on to them, even if they are promoting a high interest rate, for they might be of use in the near future.

Also remember that you cannot make transfers between identical banks; in other words, if you have a Visa Gold from Citibank, you cannot make a transfer to your Citibank Platinum, and vice versa. The lesson to learn here is: Pay attention—and be punctual!

How to Plan Ahead

Transfer checks might be handled as either cash advances or regular purchases, as was previously mentioned in "Review the Details," on page 57. It will always be in your favor that a transfer check is handled as a regular purchase (though most are not), simply because you usually end up paying less in finance charges and you avoid a lot of complications. Let's consider the implications involved when transferring balances.

✂ When the transfer checks are under the terms and conditions of a cash advance, you will want to make the transfer as late as possible. In other words, if credit card A has a balance with a payment due date of the eleventh of May, you will want to send the transfer check as close to that date as possible. Because as soon as the transfer is completed to the credit card B account, it will incur interest. (Assuming the balance in credit card A is not under agreements of a cash advance, the interest rate is equal to or less than the new offer, and that it expires on the eleventh of May.)

✂ When transferring an account that was already receiving a daily interest rate into another account with a *lower* rate, it is in your best interest to send a transfer check as soon as possible, even if the transfer is being treated as a cash advance, for the fewer number of days that a balance exists in credit card A, the more money you will save. But credit cards can be very tricky in these circumstances, especially if the interest rate is about to expire. Take a look at the following example of getting caught with a higher interest rate:

Credit card A has a balance at 8.9% (the interest is applied daily) with the closing date of April 11. Credit card B is offering a 7.9% rate for the next six months (the interest is also applied daily).

The statement of credit card A does not arrive until the eighteenth of April. If the 8.9% was a special rate that had expired on the eleventh, you'll then be paying a much higher rate, let's say 17.95%. By the time you receive the statement, you will already have owed seven days at the 17.95% rate. That might not sound like much, but if you are also unaware that your balance has been established under the terms of a cash advance, you will end up owing much more in future finance charges. You might not even be notified until your next statement that the 8.9% rate had expired, and by then you might have already accumulated thirty or more days at the 17.95% interest rate.

Do not expect a big banner in the middle of your statement announcing that the low rate has expired. It might be noted in small letters in the rate summary box, which is usually located in the lower portion of the statement. If you do not notice it, you might find yourself paying the higher rate for many months.

To make sure this situation does not happen in the future, be more aware of your balances and of the terms and conditions of the monthly finance charges. It is usually a good idea to write down whether a balance is established as either a cash advance or a purchase, to always know the exact day on which an interest rate expires, and to note that information in your "The Layout" chart (you might need to contact the credit card issuer's customer representative).

So in order to take advantage of the 7.9% interest rate offer from Credit card B without accumulating additional finance charges from Credit card A, Credit card A must receive payment on or before April 11.

Just take a look at Bob's "Notes" column in

"The Layout" chart, on page 18. For Bob's Bank One credit card, he has noted that the balance is under cash advance terms, so that when the 8.9% rate is near expiration (which he noted as March 5, 1999), he will be prepared.

Once you become accustomed to carrying out the first rule of this book—Be organized—situations such as this will no longer happen to you.

For another way to plan ahead with balance transfers, let's return to Bob's "The Layout" chart, on page 18. Notice the arrows drawn between credit cards. He has accumulated several low interest rate offers and is planning to do numerous balance transfers. Using the arrows to plan ahead, he knows immediately when a billing statement arrives if there will be a balance transfer and to what account. By following this method, you too can benefit by planning ahead of time for your balance transfers. For example, if you know in advance that your Credit card A balance will need to be transferred to your Credit card B and Credit card C accounts (both offering 6.9% rates), then you can draw arrows between the accounts on "The Layout" chart. This will save you much time and confusion, especially when transferring numerous balances at one time.

In the event you want to pay your bill in full, it is usually a good idea to call your credit card issuer for the total amount due in seven to ten days. This will enable you to be sure you cover the finance charges while the check is in the mail and being processed, which generally can take anywhere from five to ten days.

You will notice, as you do more transfers between credit cards, that you'll receive more special low interest rate offers from them. Your credit cards will be fighting each other, trying to beat each other with lower rates, attempting to get you back as their customer. They will mail you offers, call you, and in the near future might even knock at your door. Your best defense is to be prepared! Remember that credit card issuers try to make their business as tricky and complex as possible. But as long as you are prepared and organized, you will always be one step ahead.

You might wonder what happens if you have no transfer checks in the first place, or at least none that are worth using. The next section, "Calling the Credit Card Issuer," answers that question.

CALLING THE CREDIT CARD ISSUER

All individuals can benefit from calling the credit card company for lower rates. You might be surprised by what might be offered just for the asking!

You haven't received any transfer checks by mail? Perhaps the checks you've already gotten have only high interest rates? The next step is to call a credit card issuer that you wish to make a transfer to. It's also a good idea to check with *all* your credit card issuers before making any balance transfers to find out what special rates the companies are offering.

Unlike the others, Jennifer might find herself in the position of needing to call more frequently for lower rates. She does not have the "student" title of Tom, nor the credit history and number of credit cards that the Joneses and Bob have, so it's obvious that the first move is up to her.

When you do call, ask to speak to the marketing department about special balance transfer interest rates. Sometimes special rates do exist, and for whatever reason you've not been notified. Remember to make notes regarding which company offers what rate in "The Layout" chart and ask yourself the same type of questions asked in "Review the Details" (on page 57). Also make note of the date you called, so that if a few months pass and you have not heard of any special offers, you can try again. Some credit card companies are not very efficient in marketing special offers, so sometimes it requires a little work on your part.

PHONE TRANSFERS

If you are prepared to make a transfer of another balance, you can do so over the telephone, which is usually faster than waiting for any actual transfer balance checks to arrive. If you already have the checks, however, it is faster to send the balance that is to be transferred out directly to the credit card company than to call again. You only need to worry about waiting for checks to be sent to you if you have a due date to meet. For those who are in a real hurry, some balances can be transferred electronically within forty-eight hours, making it faster than any other process. It is best to check with your company's customer service representative to determine if such a service is available. In some cases, transaction fees might even be waived if a transfer is done over the phone.

Generally speaking, it does not hurt to call credit card issuers to find out about special offers. Sometimes they even have several rates being offered at one time. Chances are, however, that the customer service representative will offer you the highest rate first. So if you are offered a 9.9% interest rate for balance transfers, ask if there is anything lower—you might be surprised what other, lower balance transfer rates they have to offer. It is also true that some credit card issuers are not willing to offer lower rates. When this becomes the case, we go on to our next plan, "Calling the Credit Card Issuer on Your Terms," and take a more aggressive approach.

If you ever find yourself in a situation in which you have a total balance of $1 or less, due to finance charges, call the issuer. It should be able to waive the fee, especially if the finance charges are only a few cents.

CALLING THE CREDIT CARD ISSUER ON YOUR TERMS

*The length of time you've had the credit card, your payment history, and the amount of debt will be important factors in negotiating. Therefore, **Tom** and **Jennifer** might not have as much flexibility here. The **Joneses** and **Bob**, however, could greatly benefit from this section and should read on!*

If you're good at bluffing in poker, then calling the credit card issuer on your terms will be easy (just put on your best poker face—or, in this case, poker "voice"). There's only one thing you need to remember: You are their client, and as long as all your payments have been on time, you will be treated very well. Credit cards are represented by businesses, commercial banks and credit unions. Like other businesses, credit card issuers need clients in order to make money; if they start to treat their clients poorly, they'd lose a lot of money.

The credit card issuers also need to be flexible with their

clients, otherwise they would lose them. You can thank competition for this. If the credit card you had was the only one in the world, do you think you'd be treated as well? In today's world, there are thousands of credit cards to choose from, over ten thousand credit card issuers, and interest rates ranging from 4.9% to 24%. The credit card issuers know this, and now so do you. They don't want to see you use another credit card.

As in many worlds, seniority has its privileges. Since Bob has had three of his credit cards for more than fifteen years with an outstanding payment history, he will be able to use his seniority to his advantage.

PLAY YOUR CARDS RIGHT

This system of dealing with credit cards on your terms works only with cards that already have a balance. You need a balance to bluff with, since you'll be claiming that another credit card is offering you a better rate. Chances are the credit card issuer will believe you, because many special low-rate offers are sent out every day, though if you're currently paying a 4.9% interest rate and you claim that you have been offered a better rate, your chances will be very slim of getting a lower rate. As with poker, one needs to play with odds: The higher the rate on your credit card balance, the better your chances of getting a lower rate. Also, if you've already done many balance transfers with the credit card, the higher your odds. Always remember that lowering your rates is something you'll be able to do over and over again.

You now know what is required, what needs to be done, and how to do it when calling the credit card issuer. But what exactly does one say? What follows are "The Words of Power"—what to say when negotiating.

THE WORDS OF POWER

"I recently received a competitive interest rate offer from another credit card. I would like to know if the interest on my current balance could either be matched or lowered. If not, I will have to transfer this balance." (Be prepared to say what the other interest rate is, or even give the name of another credit card. Remember, you are bluffing!)

"I am leaving the country in a month and I just happened to notice that the special rate I have will soon expire. Currently I am cutting down my payments and I will need to transfer this balance. Unless, of course, you would be willing to lower the rate." (They might ask you to what country you're going, just to be courteous.)

"I would like to have a better interest rate applied to my balance. I have been a relatively good customer by always paying at least the required amount. I feel it is unfair to charge me the same interest rate that would be charged to a more irresponsible customer." (This is the honest approach.)

These are only a few samples, but a few well-chosen words can be surprisingly effective. How many times will you call that one credit card company? With "The Words of Power," you will only need to call once and the interest rate on your balance will be lowered, unless the company is poorly managed and is willing to risk losing you as a customer.*

---

*What if you've already called and they've lowered your interest rate, but that was six months ago and the rate is soon to expire? Well, you might want to confront the credit card issuer once again. It would be best to see if the interest rate could be extended, and you can accomplish this by saying: "Is there any way to extend the special interest rate offer I currently have, so I do not have to go through the hassle of transferring my balance to a lower interest rate on another credit card?"

If the credit card is represented by a large institution, chances are you will be transferred to the marketing department. If by chance you are transferred to the customer service department instead, ask to be transferred to marketing. The customer service representative might be unable to handle your request.

If, for some reason, when you are employing "The Words of Power," the customer representative is not buying your bluff or does not have the authority to do what you wish, ask to speak to his or her superior. Chances are the superior will be more knowledgeable and will have the authorization to give you a lower interest rate. If for some reason he or she doesn't, attempt to convince him or her that it would be better for the company to make 5.9% interest on your balance than 0% interest, since you will be transferring the balance.

There are some cases when your interest rate cannot be lowered. That is the time to ask if it is possible to actually move that account to another credit card that has a special low introductory rate and is represented by the same issuer. Sometimes even upgrading your account to a gold or platinum card will give you access to a low introductory interest rate. Such an upgrade, however, would depend on how good a customer you have been and for how long. It's unlikely that the credit card issuer will be flexible if you have been a member for only a few months or haven't always paid your bills on time.

Tom, for example, has had his credit cards for less than nine months, and even though he has always made his payments, he would not be considered a candidate for a significant upgrade (basic card to platinum card) mainly because of his "high risk" status (See "How You Compare to the Joneses," on page 119) and low income.

But if you are a hardworking, hard-paying consumer, remember that "The Words of Power" have proved very effective. You are encouraged to use them after following all other recommended procedures. It's also important to remember that credit card companies *can* be flexible, especially when it comes to keeping their clients. They might not like giving you a lower rate, but most often they will. That same credit card issuer might also think that after a certain promotion ends, it'll be able to catch you with a higher rate. But as long as you stay organized and prepared, you will be able to avoid such interest rate hikes.

Whether you transfer your balance by mail or phone, it will be worth your time and effort because "The Words of Power" will most likely result in lowering your interest rate. The following chart shows how you can truly save from decreasing the cost of your credit card debt. (NOTE: the interest applied represents twelve months. For a more accurate interest rate comparison chart, make sure to see "The Interest Comparison Chart," on page 197.)

Compare Those Rates!

Balance	18.9%	11.9%	5.9%
$ 1,000.00	$ 189.00	$ 119.00	$ 59.00
$ 2,000.00	$ 378.00	$ 238.00	$ 118.00
$ 3,000.00	$ 567.00	$ 357.00	$ 177.00
$ 4,000.00	$ 756.00	$ 476.00	$ 236.00
$ 5,000.00	$ 945.00	$ 595.00	$ 295.00
$ 6,000.00	$ 1,134.00	$ 714.00	$ 354.00
$ 7,000.00	$ 1,323.00	$ 833.00	$ 413.00
$ 8,000.00	$ 1,512.00	$ 952.00	$ 472.00
$ 9,000.00	$ 1,701.00	$ 1,071.00	$ 531.00
$ 10,000.00	$ 1,890.00	$ 1,190.00	$ 590.00

Unfortunately, some credit card issuers still won't budge on interest rates no matter what. Generally these tend to be smaller companies. But there is no need to worry, because if credit card A doesn't lower your rates, credit card B might be more than happy to. If your credit card issuers tend to be inflexible with their interest rates, you might just want to apply for some other credit cards that are more flexible. This idea of flexibility leads us to our next section, "The More, the Merrier."

THE MORE, THE MERRIER

It was previously mentioned in "What Lies Ahead," (page 4) that you should not cancel any credit cards in the midst of your debt reduction process. The reason for that is because the more credit cards you use, the more special low interest rate offers you will receive. In turn, you will have more room to move your debts around. Your flexibility rating, as was mentioned on page 45, will be higher the more credit cards you have. One negative aspect of having many credit cards is that it doesn't look good on your credit report.

Unless you plan to apply for loans during your credit card debt reduction, it is recommended that you keep all the credit cards until your balances are down to 10%—or less—of your original credit card debt. In the battle against credit cards, one might think that by simply reducing the number of credit cards he or she is winning the war. The opposite, in fact, is true: The cost of your debt (the interest rate) has better odds of decreasing with eight credit cards than with two.

Take, for example, the Joneses. Even though they are in deep water with credit card debt and have a low flexibility rating, they do have one strong advantage: twelve credit cards, which will give them the opportunity to significantly lower the cost of their debt.

LISTEN CLOSELY

The world is not perfect and neither are credit cards. Sometimes what seems clear is not clear at all. So here is one final bit of advice: When you are speaking to a customer service representative, listen closely to the way he or she answers your questions.

For example, a customer service representative might tell you that you *should* not be charged any fees for the transfer of a particular balance. After hearing the word *should,* your attention is called for. If he or she then tells you that you can always call back and have any fees removed if you are charged, make sure to get his or her name! But it is best to speak to a supervisor before going ahead with the process if the customer service representative is unsure of any transaction. The last thing you want is to pay additional costs because of a customer service representative's uncertainty.

Whether receiving a very unique offer or resolving a previous problem on the telephone, always make sure to note the representative's full name, the department that individual worked in, and the date and time. This is very important for your protection in the event you do not actually receive the special offer and/or an error is not resolved regarding your account.

Congratulations! You have now come to the end of the first part of the book! You have learned the basics of controlling your credit card debt, how to save money, and most important, how to stay away from the traps and tricks of the credit card companies. You will now be able to lower those dreadful interest rates and start saving a lot of money. You will notice that as the interest rates go down and your payments continue, your credit card debt will decrease faster and faster because less money will be going toward the interest and more toward the balance.

But you can save even more! The following chapters are as essential as these were in learning to not only lower but completely eradicate your credit card debt. So continue reading on as more mysterious aspects of the credit card phenomenon unfold.

Part Two

A Few Signs on

the Highway

What You Need to Know

Having completed Part One, you have now accomplished the three most important steps toward organizing, analyzing, and reducing your credit card debt and should now be seeing positive results as your debt decreases. We now move on to other essential methods that will help you reduce your credit card debt even further, as well as some eye-opening facts that might prove useful for credit card users.

MINIMUM PAYMENT—TRICKS OF THE TRADE

*This is one of the most important sections in this book and so applies to **all individuals**. If you are only paying the minimum amount due, then you need to read this section.*

The minimum payment is, perhaps, the most misunderstood aspect of credit cards. Many consumers think that all they have to pay is the minimum amount due each month and they will get out of debt. Although that might be true, it will take many years, especially if someone is playing by the credit card issuer's rules. Credit card debt takes three times as long to pay off as any conventional loan. A balance that was originally $3,000 might end up costing $10,000 to pay off. This is why, perhaps, credit cards are the most profitable form of banking, even with so many individuals not paying their bills and still others filing for bankruptcy.

Credit card issuers determine the minimum amount due in several ways: by taking a percentage of your balance, such as 2%, or by dividing your balance by a certain number of months, such as forty-eight (which does not necessarily mean that the owed amount will be paid off in forty-eight months, especially if most of your payments are going toward your monthly finance charges). In order to find out how yours has been determined, you will have to call customer service, or you can look for the pamphlet that was sent to you when you opened the account, which most likely has met its destiny in your trash container ages ago.

One factor that must be remembered is that the credit card company has calculated the minimum payments in its best interest, not yours. This chapter will teach you to ignore its rules and suggestions and to follow the suggestions in this book.

> *For many credit card issuers, the* favorite *customer is the one who pays only the minimum due.*

RULE #1—DON'T PAY THE MINIMUM

As the months go by and you are making payments, you will notice that the minimum payment amount decreases. If you are currently making only minimum payments, then the decrease might be just a few dollars a month. In the long term, these small amounts add up; but it still might take you years to get out of debt. The best alternative, if you can afford to do so, is to pay a fixed amount every month. Let's say your minimum payment for the first month is $100; you should continue to send that amount each subsequent month. The next minimum will perhaps be around $95, and if you are paying a continuous $100, your debt will decrease at a faster rate. If possible, start with a larger amount, such as $110, but choose an amount that you can stick with every month.

It is also a good idea to prioritize your payments. Even after lowering the interest rates on all your credit cards, some rates will still be higher than others. Therefore, apply larger additional payments, above the minimum, to higher interest rate cards than to those with lower interest rates.

Bob, for example, is a step ahead. He has paid more than the minimum due each month, and has also prioritized his payments, as can be seen in the "Pay" column in his "The Details" chart, on page 28. By carrying out these two important steps, he has kept the effect of compounding interest to a minimum, especially once he significantly lowered his average interest rate of 17.35% (see "A Wise Choice," on page 89).

You can accomplish the same results Bob has achieved! Armed with this information, it is now time to organize and prioritize your payments.

First, you need to organize your credit cards. Rank them from highest to lowest interest rate on a separate piece of paper.

Next, as you did in "Categorize Your Credit Cards," on page 49, you will need to separate them into three groups of high (15% and above), medium (14.9% to 9.5%), and low (9.4% or below) interest rates.

Finally, try to set an amount to pay over the minimums due. Remember that this figure will vary according to interest rates and especially when doing numerous balance transfers. Therefore, establish an amount that you can afford to pay extra each month toward *all* your credit cards, whether it's $25 or $300. This amount will be divided among your credit cards and will be added on to the already required minimum payments. Take a look at how Jennifer handled this situation after she had lowered the interest rate on her three credit cards:

Prioritizing Payments

- ✂ Jennifer has three credit cards, each with a different interest rate: 7.9%, 6.9%, and 5.9%.
- ✂ She can spend an additional $110 a month toward her credit cards.
- ✂ The minimum payments for this month are $50 for the 7.9% card, $45 for the 6.9% card, and $20 for the 5.9% card.
- ✂ She will distribute the additional $110 in the following manner: $95 for the 7.9% card, $10 for the 6.9% card, and $5 for the 5.9% card. (See the following chart.)

Interest	Minimum Due	Additional	Total Per Month
7.90%	$ 50.00	$ 95.00	$145.00
6.90%	$ 45.00	$ 10.00	$ 55.00
5.90%	$ 20.00	$ 5.00	$ 25.00

As long as Jennifer continuously stays with this payment plan, her credit card debt will decrease at a faster rate. If you follow the same method as Jennifer, your debt will also decease accordingly. Of course, you can also apply a large sum to the credit card with the highest interest rate at any time, but that takes all the fun out of it. At the very least, remember to always pay slightly more than the minimum payment, regardless of the interest rate.*

---

*Some credit card issuers track whether a cardholder pays only the minimum due on a regular basis, usually for marketing purposes or sometimes to help evaluate the risk of an individual. If a cardholder is considered a high-

A WISE CHOICE

Take a look at the sample for "The Monthly Checkup" chart, on page 42. Bob has paid $585 every month to all his credit cards. He was able to lower the average interest rate from 17.35% to nearly 6.5%. The actual total of all minimum amounts due in September 1998 was $418, in August 1999, it was $323. But by paying $585 a month and lowering the interest rate, he was able to reduce his debt by almost $4,800 for the year and clear three credit cards. If Bob had not paid a constant amount and had not lowered the interest rates, he would have reduced his credit card debt by only about $1,300. He would also have paid about $1,770 more in interest. For a further detailed look at how he and the other characters reduced their credit card debt, take a look at "Five Smiling Faces," on page 179.

RULE #2—NEVER SKIP A PAYMENT

If you have an excellent payment history, credit card issuers will sometimes offer you the opportunity to skip a monthly payment. Unless you simply can't afford to pay that month, stick with the fixed amount you've established to pay monthly as explained in Rule #1. Keep in mind that finance charges will still apply for that month whether you pay or not. If you choose not to pay, your balance will actu-

---

er risk than when he or she first applied for the credit card, he or she might be required to pay a higher interest rate or even lose benefits, such as exemption from future line-of-credit increases. By paying slightly above the minimum, you avoid falling in the category of "only paying the minimum due."

ally increase, and you might end up with the balance you'd had the previous month or two, depending, of course, on the interest rate and balance. Although this offer might seem inviting, it is really just another trick to help keep you a long-time customer.

Want to reduce your credit card debt even faster? Instead of sending your fixed amount each month to your creditor, send half of your usual monthly payment every two weeks. This step will save you money by reducing the monthly finance charge. And for your convenience, see if the creditor can receive automatic payment through your checking account (do this only if you do not plan to transfer balances in—or out—of the account anytime soon).

RULE #3—DON'T JUST PAY THE INTEREST

Take a look at the finance charge that applies on each month's statement. How large is it compared to your minimum payment? Sometimes if the interest rate is very high, the finance charge can equal—or even be higher than—your minimum payment. If this happens, you can be sure your debt will increase. You can avoid this situation once you have lowered the interest rates on your credit cards, because you never want to pay just the interest on your credit card. See the following example of a $2,000 balance with an interest rate of 23% and a minimum payment configuration of 2%.

$38.33   Finance Charge $40.00   Minimum Due

$2,000 + $38.33 - $40.00 = $1998.33

So you end up paying only $1.67 of your outstanding balance. Just imagine the long-term effect!

RULE #4—A TRANSFER IS NOT A PAYMENT

Even when making a balance transfer you should not forget to continue paying the minimum payment, at the very least. For example, if you are planning on transferring your remaining balance of $2,300 and the regular monthly amount you pay is $100, then transfer $2,200 and write a personal check for $100.*

In Bob's "The Transfer" chart, on page 37, you can see that when he transferred his balances for lower interest rates (Bank Two to Bank Six), he also made sure to pay his regular monthly payment of $100 to Bank Two, as noted in the "Pay" column in his "The Details" chart, on page 28.

The method works either through the mail or through a customer service representative. If done by phone, you will only need to send your regular payment and the transfer will be taken care of. However, if done by mail, you will need to send at least two checks to the credit card issuer. When you start to do numerous transfers, it can be tempting to stop paying the minimum due. (When in a tight financial situation, you can avoid paying the minimum due, see "Unique Options," on page 142.) If the total amount of payments to your credit cards is $750 a month, then you

---

*Do not forget to write the totals of your check amounts in the "Payment Amount Enclosed" box on the payment stub when sending your payment. For example, if you have three checks—one personal and two transfers— make sure to write the total of the three in the appropriate place.

know that with all transfers and personal checks being made, this amount should be reached every month. It is important to stay constant with your payments, as you will soon see for yourself.

RULE #5—TRICK OR TREAT

Sometimes credit card issuers make special offers in which there are no payments and no finance charges for six months or more—if you use the credit card for a specific transaction. If you are planning to pay in full within six months, or plan to transfer the amount to another credit card with a low rate, that's an inviting offer. Otherwise, stay away! Once you read the fine print, you might find that the interest rate rises very high—22% or more is common—at the end of the six-month offer. What is even worse is that if the balance is not paid in full within the six months, the finance charges that were not applied during those previous six months might be applied at the 22% (or higher rate) on your next billing statement. Ultimately, your credit card debt can suddenly increase by several hundred dollars, depending on the amount of the original purchase. Trick for you, treat for them . . .

By following the rules set forth here, your debt will decrease faster and faster. Having learned how to lower your interest rates and avoid the minimum payment trap, you're now aware of the two most important factors in conquering your credit card debt. With these skills, you will no longer be taken advantage of by credit card companies.

But sure enough, if it's not through high interest rates or lucrative minimum payments, credit card issuers are still able to profit from unwary cardholders, such as through membership fees, which leads us into our next section, "How to Avoid Paying Annual Fees."

> *A sure way to not get over your head in credit card debt is to use your checking account booklet. Every time you make a purchase with your credit card, note the transaction in your checking account (as if you have already written the check). That way, when your credit card bill arrives you will have enough funds in your checking account to cover the entire bill.*

HOW TO AVOID PAYING ANNUAL FEES

Most credit card issuers do not apply annual fees to certain individuals, such as those who would not accept a credit card because of an annual fee. **Tom** *and* **Jennifer***, therefore, usually do not have to deal with annual fees. The* **Joneses** *and* **Bob***, on the other hand, might encounter cards that have annual fees and should certainly know how to deal with them.*

A small but significant factor toward winning the credit card war is learning to deal with annual fees. Annual fees are almost as flexible as the interest rates you pay on your balances. Generally speaking, credit cards with high interest rates do not have membership fees, but those with average to low fixed interest rates do. Some companies even charge a membership fee if you do not make a minimum number of purchases within the year on their credit card. Also, depending on the type of credit card you have, there might be a high annual fee. For example, a gold card frequently has a higher annual fee than a basic card. Usually, credit cards with standard low fixed interest rates will not be very flexible with annual fees, simply because they feel that since they are offering terms with a low fixed interest rate, they should be able to charge an annual fee. This trend, however, is declining, and fewer credit cards are charging annual fees.

> *Probably the best way—and the only guaranteed way—to avoid paying annual fees is to have a credit card with no annual fee to begin with.*

This is great news for people like the Joneses, who have twelve credit cards, seven of which have annual fees totaling $200 a year. When the Joneses applied for their credit cards in the early 1980s, annual fees were common. Now, however, many credit card rules have changed, mostly because of competition and consumer demand.

Annual fees are a great way for credit card companies to pull in extra revenue. Most often, misinformed consumers feel that they have no choice but to pay annual fees, especially if they have a balance they are unable to pay off or transfer. You might be tempted at this point to simply cancel any credit cards without balances, but maintaining several credit cards can be very practical, unless a certain credit card is absolutely worthless and there is an annual fee. For example, if you have a credit card you never use, with a high interest rate that is never flexible, a low credit limit that has no hope of increasing, *and* an annual fee, that might be the right card to cancel. Say the credit card has a limit of $500 and an annual fee of $25; that $25 can be considered as 5% interest on a balance you do not even have.

Take a moment to review any accounts that might be similar to this example and consider canceling them before you are charged the next annual fee.

Besides cancellation, there are other methods for avoiding annual fees for those who have no balances—as well as for those who do. Let's read on and learn the unique techniques for blocking the annual fee.

WITHOUT A BALANCE

To bluff or not to bluff. The choice is yours. For those without a balance, simply call the credit card company and say that because of the annual fee you want to cancel the account. Remember that you can do this only with a zero balance.

Depending on its policy and your payment history, the company might be willing to cancel the annual fee for that year, or at least meet you halfway by reducing it. If it does not and there is no need for the credit card, then cancel the account. After doing so, you might be lucky and soon receive a letter (or call) saying that the annual fee has been canceled and the account can be re-opened, if you wish to reconsider. However, if you truly need the credit card, and your bluffing did not work, it is best to say that you will call back later to handle the transaction, which, of course, you will not do.

WITH A BALANCE

For those who do carry a balance and do have a significant amount of credit available, the approach, and the bluff, would be different. Instead of saying you intend to cancel the credit card, you can tell the customer service representative that you'd be willing to transfer more money to the credit card if they'd cancel the annual fee. Otherwise, you might tell them that you're planning to transfer the current amount and close the account. If the credit card issuer wants to continue making money, it'd be wise to accept such terms, simply because the annual fee can never compare to the amount of revenue brought in by interest rates.

Fees Credit Card Issuers Like to Charge

- Finance fee
- Annual fee
- Cash advance fee
- Over-the-credit-limit fee
- Late payment fee
- Declined check fee
- Stop payment fee
- Research fee
- Copying (statement/sales slip) fee

Throughout this book, it has been emphasized that you are engaged in a battle against the possible evils of credit cards. You want to approach the battle in a diplomatic manner. It is never a good idea to be too defensive or too aggressive in a situation that requires negotiation and whose end is to save you money. By being polite, you will greatly increase the odds of saving money in any type of situation you might encounter with your credit cards!

With your annual fee now only a memory, we move forward and learn how and why increasing your credit limit—oddly enough—can assist you in your credit card battles.

THE SKY'S THE LIMIT

*Increasing the credit limit for **Tom** and **Jennifer** will only increase their purchasing power, therefore such an action would be dangerous. But for other more responsible individuals such as the **Joneses** and **Bob**, an increase in the* *credit limit can be a lifesaver in the long run. For those of you who like to consume: Stay away from this section!*

Your credit limit is the amount of credit that is available to you on your credit card. It usually grows according to your payment history, the policy of the credit card issuer, and the type of credit card. You probably think of it as purchasing power, which you should not. Think of it as transferring power, because the higher your limit, the more you'll be able to take advantage of a lower interest rate, resulting in a lower average interest rate on your total credit card debt. As you increase the number of credit cards and are responsible with them, your total credit limit can increase almost indefinitely.

Tom's and Jennifer's spending power can be reflected from their credit card limits. If they are not careful, they might end up with much larger balances. Tom has a total credit limit of $1,000 between his two cards, therefore the $1,000 is the maximum amount of credit card debt he can accumulate at any one time. Since he carries a relatively small balance of $319.76 and a flexibility rating of 3.13, he is in good shape. But this can all change if his credit limits are increased. The Joneses, on the other hand, have a total balance of $45,127.32 and a total limit of $49,000. With a flexibility rating of only 1.08, it is vital that they try to increase their credit limit to help lower their overall average interest rate. (Remember the flexibility rating?—the ratio that determined how flexible your credit card debt would be (see page 45)? Your credit limit has an effect on your flexibility rating, and every time your credit limit increases, so will your overall flexibility rating!)

WHAT DETERMINES YOUR LIMIT

Credit card issuers look at several prospects during certain periods and ultimately decide on whether to increase credit limits. They review your payment history, attentive to such matters as whether you've paid each statement on time and the payment amounts (minimum or payment in full). They might review your credit history to see how you are doing with other credit cards, and take into account how long you've been their customer and when the last credit limit increase was made. The review might include charting your spending habits and exact use of the credit card: whether you never use it, are often near your credit limit, or often exceed the limit. Additionally, the type of credit card will determine the limit you are eligible for. Generally speaking, there are four classes: basic, silver, gold, and platinum. Each has a maximum possible credit limit. A basic card could have a maximum limit of $1,000, while a platinum card could have a maximum limit of $100,000.* Of course, all this depends on the actual credit card issuer. If you have a platinum card, however, the chances are higher that you will get a larger credit increase than with a basic card. Some banks will even upgrade your credit card (go from silver to gold) in order to give you a higher credit limit.

As you can see, there are many ways in which credit card companies review your status as a customer. Continue reading to discover the two rules that you should follow in order to receive improved credit limits in the future.

---

*Even though credit card issuers have advertised platinum credit cards with $100,000 limits, I have yet to know someone who carries such a card.

RULE #1—KEEP AN EYE ON IT

Never exceed your credit limit and never get too close to it. Know your limit as stated in your "The Layout" chart. One common mistake that leads to exceeding limits is miscalculating balance transfers. If you know approximately what your next finance charge will be, double that amount, for that is how much away from your limit you should stay. Otherwise, you might exceed the limit with the finance charge. For example: Your limit is $4,000, with a balance of $2,000 If you were to transfer an additional $2,000 to your balance and the finance charge were $23 on the following statement, your outstanding balance would be $4,023. You would have exceeded the limit of $4,000, which would be a negative mark for you.*

However, if you applied the "double finance charge" rule and had transferred only $1,954 ($2,000 - $23 × 2 = $1,954), the balance would have been $3,954. With the next finance charge of $23 this would bring you to $3,977.** You do not need to be exact in determining your next finance charge, and chances are you will not be, because there are other factors that apply along with the interest rate that you may or may not be aware of, such as the "Balance Configurations" on page 102, which may only result in a difference of a few dollars. That is why you should double your estimate, just to be safe. Such moves will save you from getting an unnecessary negative mark with your credit card.

---

*To figure an approximation of your future finance charge, divide the current APR (in this case, 6.9%) by 12 and then multiply that by the total balance, including the transferred balance—.069 / 12 months = .00575, then .00575 × $4,000.00 = $23.00.

**Actually, the finance charge would be slightly less than $23, since only $1,954 had been transferred—rather than $2,000—and the finance charge would be determined by a balance of $3,954, instead of $4,000. The final balance would then be slightly less than $3,977.

RULE #2—BE PUNCTUAL

Always pay on time and, if possible, pay more than the minimum due, as explained in "Rule #1—Don't Pay the Minimum." When you receive a statement, do not wait to send the payment a few days before it is due if you can send it right away.* Paying the due amount, and paying it on time at the very least, shows that you are responsible. A credit card issuer is certainly not going to increase your limit if you cannot even handle the limit you currently have.

> *Another reason for paying on time: If your account ever goes into default, the credit card issuer might increase your account's APR—simply because you are now perceived as a riskier borrower.*

Throughout this book, it has been shown how credit card issuers make huge profits from charging cardholders high interest rates, a fact that can never be overemphasized. But did you know that there are different ways in which credit cards can charge you interest on your balance? The answer lies in the next section, "Interest, Interest, and Interest."

---

*In terms of transferring balances, properly timing your payment and transfer can be crucial in saving money. For more details, see "How to Plan Ahead," on page 69.

INTEREST, INTEREST, AND INTEREST

*This is an important section for **all individuals** to review simply because no one is dealing with "interest-free" credit card debt.*

You are well aware that you will pay interest on your credit card debt, but did you know that a 5.9% interest rate can cost you more on one card than on another with the same interest rate?

"Interest, Interest, and Interest" enumerates the three most important concepts to remember about credit cards. Credit card issuers make money from interest, and you, in turn, lose money. They want the interest rate to be as high as possible, and you want it to be as low as possible. They want the high rate applied for as lengthy a period as possible, which will result in a shorter grace period, while you want the longest possible grace period. Without interest rates, credit cards would cease to exist. Without interest rates, you would not have found yourself in credit card debt in the first place. In fact, you probably wouldn't have been in debt at all, since it's unlikely that someone sensibly minded would have loaned you money without being able to apply interest.

It's also true that credit card issuers would never let you pay minimum payments in installments without interest because they'd be the ones losing money. Since interest rates are generally the major cost of your debt, what you have to do is keep those rates down to begin winning the battle. Though there are other things that will lower your credit card debt, nothing has as much effect as lowering your interest rates. Even after credit card companies apply a specific interest rate to your balance, terms and conditions might apply that require you to pay more than you thought you would.

The following section illustrates the three ways in which credit card issuers calculate your balance in order to apply their finance charges.

BALANCE CONFIGURATIONS

1. Adjusted Balance—The adjusted balance is calculated by subtracting any credits or payments made during the current billing cycle from the balance from the previous billing cycle. Purchases made during the current billing cycle will not be included. By the end of the cycle, therefore, whichever part of the balance is paid will not be accompanied by a finance charge.

2. Average Daily Balance—In order to figure your balance due, the credit card issuer will take your total balance each day and deduct any payments or credits received that day. Then all the daily balances are added together and divided by the number of days in the billing cycle, which results in your average daily balance. Depending on each issuer's policy, new purchases might or might not be added to the average daily balance. If they are, however, that generally means there is no grace period on new purchases and you pay interest as soon as the purchase is made. Cash advances are usually added to the average daily balance and generally accrue interest as soon as the transaction is made.

3. Previous Balance—Your previous balance is simply the balance that is owed from the previous billing cycle. Any credits, payments, or purchases made within the current billing cycle will not be taken into account.

If those three methods sound confusing, they are supposed to! If you've ever seen one of the creditors' pamphlets referring to how the finance charges are computed, you know it can look like it's written in another language. Credit card issuers generally do not make it easy for you to see their maneuvers.

Not only do they want to get interest from you, they want as much of that interest as possible. Take a look at the following simplified examples of the three balance configurations.

With a balance of $1,000, an APR of 19.2%, and a one-month payment of $300, these are the finance charges that would result from using each of the three different balance configurations.

1. Adjusted Balance—Finance Charge = $11.20.
2. Average Daily Balance—Finance Charge = $13.60.
3. Previous Balance—Finance Charge = $16.

From this information, we can see that the adjusted balance is the most advantageous to consumers—and it happens to be the least common method used by credit card issuers. The previous balance, obviously, is the most advantageous to credit card issuers.

This information will be useful to you in the event you ever come up with two credit cards with the same interest rates and the exact same balances, yet the finance charges are different. Also be sure to review the back of your monthly statements to see how the balance is configured, since it is required by law for the credit card issuers to show this information.

You now know more than credit card issuers would ever expect a cardholder to know—a tremendous disadvantage to them and another battle won by you in the credit card war. Let's go to the following section, which depicts the different roles cash advances play for consumers and credit card issuers.

CASH ADVANCE—FRIEND OR FOE?

*Almost every credit card has a pin number. Therefore, **all
individuals** are endangered by using their credit cards
improperly. Read this if you are unfamiliar with taking cash
advances from your credit card.*

Cash advances are very advantageous to credit card
companies. They often charge a fee for accessing the cash,
the cash is almost always tied to a very high interest rate,
and the interest rate is always applied daily. Sometimes,
however, there are special low cash advance rates, and
you should check your statement to see what rate applies.
The fee for cash advances is usually around 2% of the balance, but no more than a fixed amount—such as $20—
will be charged.* If the interest rate is low and is offered
for a long period of time, and if you're lucky enough to
avoid a transaction fee, an advance might be to *your* best
advantage.

Cash advances can occasionally be lifesavers for those
short on cash. Since there are still many payees who do not
accept credit cards for payment—landlords, utility companies, colleges, and others**—you can always pay with a
cash advance check from a credit card if need be. This
scenario should occur only in emergency cases, because if
you were to become accustomed to using such methods,
you might pay a fortune in cash advance fees, very high

---

*Borrower beware—some credit card issuers charge a cash advance fee of
at least $3 or 3%, or even more. Therefore, an amount of $5,000 can have
a transaction fee as high as $150 (or more), something one would definite-
ly want to avoid. Because consumers have been accessing more cash
advances, credit card issuers have been taking advantage of the demand.

**Actually, colleges are now starting to accept credit cards as payment for
tuition. You might soon be able to accumulate bonus points with which to
purchase schoolbooks. Now, there's an incentive to study harder!

interest rates, and your debt would most definitely increase.

In Jennifer's case, her pin number gave her access to using cash advances excessively. In the past year alone, she withdrew a combined $2,000 from ATMs, costing her an average 24% in finance charges. Though she now pays an average 18.72%, some of that still reflects past cash advances.

Unfortunately, lower rates are more often offered for balance transfers than for cash advances. Therefore, if you urgently need a cash advance, but it is linked to a high interest rate, make sure to transfer that balance as soon as possible to a credit card with a special low balance transfer rate, so you'll avoid paying ridiculously high interest rates on the cash advance.*

Since many transfers are considered cash advances, there might or might not be a fee involved. But the interest rate will be applied daily—unlike a regular balance transfer that might have a grace period—which means you will pay a bit more in finance charges. Depending on the situation, it might, or might not, be worth it. For further information on how credit card companies take advantage of cash advance terms and how to prepare for them, read "How to Plan Ahead," on page 69, if you haven't done so already.

Cash advances can also be used for investment purposes. If a rate is low and you feel you can use the money to make an investment with a higher return, such a transaction can be very profitable. This kind of manipulation

---

*NOTE: Some credit card accounts do not allow you to access your full credit limit as a cash advance, so check your statement. Usually, if there is a specific limitation to cash advances, it will be noted there. It's also a good idea to make a note of such circumstances in the "Notes" column of "The Layout" chart for those accounts, which will ensure that you don't accidentally exceed your cash advance limit.

should be practiced only by those with experience in investing with borrowed money, since a cash advance always needs to be paid back! The cash advance will also increase your credit card debt. So unless you know what you are getting yourself into, stay clear from this concept. If your investment fails, remember that you will be in deeper debt than before.

Bob saw an opportunity that he felt he could not miss, so as any savvy investor might do, he applied leverage by using those credit cards that offered him the money he would otherwise not have. He thought he was getting a great deal, since two of his credit cards were offering a special 5.9% rate with no cash advance fees. Since the investment was predicted to return at least 30% for the year, he felt that he could easily cover the costs of his credit cards and make a nice profit of around 24.1% (30% - 5.9% = 24.1%). But when his investment lost 70% of its initial value and the special 5.9% rate expired with a new rate of 17%, he no longer saw his credit cards as a great deal but as a tremendous financial burden.

Investing with borrowed money, therefore, should be approached cautiously. It's not recommended for those who cannot handle risk, who already have a large amount of credit card debt, or who are unfamiliar with investing.

Generally speaking, cash advances are best used to transfer balances and nothing else. When you receive a balance transfer check whose terms and conditions match those of a cash advance, consider using it, especially if the interest rate is very low and there are no transaction fees. Even if the interest is being applied daily, as long as the interest is at least less than what you are paying on another credit card, you will save money in the long run by using it.

You now know "What You Need to Know," for effectively reducing your credit card debt. The next chapter will give you a better general understanding of your credit cards, demonstrate how beneficial they can be, and finally, assure you that you are not alone in credit card debt.

The Plastic

PLASTIC TO SOME, GOLD TO OTHERS

*Value is in the eye of the beholder. Credit cards used responsibly can prove valuable. Even though the **Joneses** and **Bob** accumulated a large amount of credit card debt, at least they were able to benefit from a few free airline tickets, some magazines, and a box of chocolates.*

Until now, we've discovered how problematic credit cards can be. In this section, we'll focus on their benefits.

THE CONVENIENCE

Credit cards can be very useful and convenient if you use them properly, especially when you're trying to avoid carrying cash. Almost every merchant accepts at least one major credit card, making it a lot easier to eliminate the need to carry cash and the hassle of using ATM machines. Think of how often you've gone to an ATM machine outside the state where your checking account is located, and how you've been charged a fee for each withdrawal. How about the time you've wasted trying to find an ATM?

Also remember that when you pay cash, it's easy to lose track of your receipts and expenses, while many credit cards send you a convenient monthly statement. Even more importantly, perhaps, you will no longer get annoyed looks at the supermarket, as you did when there was a long line and you pulled out your checkbook.

> *Credit card companies love to offer you excuses to use your cards and checks. Here are just a few examples: "Pay Your Taxes on Time," "Enjoy the Summer Holidays," "Ease Through Christmas Shopping," and "Be Able to Cover Those Unexpected Emergencies." Just remember—check that interest rate!*

Eventually, our society will no longer use cash. Transactions will occur by credit card, debit card, or other means that will not involve the hand-to-hand exchange of cash. Ever since the introduction of credit cards—accelerating in the 1980s and 1990s—the exchange of cash has decreased in the United States while the usage of credit cards has increased, so you might as well get used to using them. Just be sure to use them infrequently until you're out of debt!

A Sense of Security

Another benefit of credit cards is that if ever you were to lose your card, you are by law liable only for purchases up to $50.* Since credit cards are always checked for validity, a low rate of illegal usage exists (as opposed to earlier times, when comparison of your signature to that on the card proved whether or not the credit card was

---

*Actually, your liability depends on how soon you report an illegal transaction. For further details on credit card liability, see "Know Your Rights," on page 163.

valid).** Compare that to losing cash, which is simply gone! Credit cards even provide you with a sense of security when making purchases with extended protection plans, and with protection against fraud and theft. Travel accident and auto rental insurance are other common benefits. So, although the credit card can be your worst enemy at times, it can be a very valuable asset if used properly.

GIVE ME THOSE POINTS

These days, one of your credit card's greatest benefits might be the "point" system it offers. Because of competition, credit card issuers have been forced to offer such benefits as free airline tickets, hotel accommodations, gasoline, Internet service, magazines, and much more. These can be thought of as usage incentives, because these companies want you to consume with their cards, over and over again. Before doing so, it is only sensible to investigate the particular benefits, or "points" that each credit card might offer. Some cards might not even offer any benefits other than a low interest rate, which in itself is one of the best benefits.

When you investigate new credit cards, find out if what they're offering is useful to you or relates to your lifestyle. Take a look at your own cards. Are they offering anything? If so, or if you're not sure, call a customer service representative for further information. If none of your credit cards offers any benefits, make sure to check out my web site at www.creditcardfreedom.com for a list of credit cards that do. For further information on my web site, see: "The Adventure Continues Online," on page 176.

For example, why would you want free gasoline if you do

**Of course, you need to report your card lost or stolen for the validating process to be effective. Your picture on the card might reduce the risk of its being improperly used.

not have a car, or free airline tickets if you do not like to travel? You also need to consider that a free airline ticket would take a lot more points to achieve than a gallon of free gasoline. It's a good idea to calculate ahead of time if you would be able to accumulate enough points to receive a free airline ticket or any other benefit so that it really *would* benefit you. It is also very important to find out if there is an expiration date for your points. The last thing you would want is to accumulate almost enough points for a trip to Mexico only to find out the next day that they have all expired.

Unfortunately, most credit cards do not offer points for transferring balances. Points are relative to a specified dollar amount that you spend on your credit card. For example, you might receive ten points for every $100 spent on a particular credit card. Each credit card has a different proportional amount.

> *Want a lot of perks—such as lost luggage protection, travel accident insurance, rental insurance, extended warranties, and roadside assistance? Then get a platinum card—they generally have the most rewarding benefits.*

The most likely question you are probably asking yourself is: Since most balance transfers do not accumulate points, how does one avoid accumulating debt and receive points at the same time? By being smart and very responsible! One method is to pay whatever regular monthly expenses you have with your credit card. Almost every merchant accepts credit cards, and it is in your best interest to pay with a credit card that offers you points toward a future benefit.

The trick is to pay the amount due in full when the next

credit card statement arrives. The figure might seem large at first, but you should realize that you would have spent the same amount in smaller increments throughout the month. Purchases you might have made by check or cash, such as your food expenses, would instead be made by credit card, and you would receive points for each dollar spent. It would also be more convenient to write one check a month rather than several checks. Since banks sometimes charge for each check you write, you're saving even more money! By following this method you can accumulate hundreds or even thousands of points a year, at the same time saving on check fees from your bank.

In order to pay all regular expenses with your credit card, remember that you must pay the balance in full every month so that no finance charges apply. Try not to make extra purchases; although they're tempting, they can be consequential. It is best to use one card continuously that has no previous balance so that when your monthly statement arrives you know that the bill must be paid in full. However, if the credit card you wish to use already has a balance that you are paying on a regular monthly basis, make sure you pay at least the minimum due as well as the amount of the purchases most recently made. For example, if the minimum due is $90 and your recent purchases totaled $300, then you need to pay at least $390.*

In accumulating points, Tom can most definitely benefit from the monthly income he receives from his parents. Instead of using cash, he can use his credit card to accumulate points to take advantage of special products and ser-

---

*You need to be very cautious in using a credit card for purchases when there is already a balance on the card, especially if there are different interest rates for purchases, cash advances, and transfers. Even if you pay the amount you spent in a particular month, your payment might be distributed between the two balances and you might be trapped into paying a very high interest rate. If this situation does not sound familiar, take a look back at "Paying Two Rates for One Balance?" on page 58.

vices offered by the credit card issuer. As long as he pays in full each month, accumulating points will cost him nothing.

Many debt counselors would not recommend using your credit card for regular purchases. This is because many cardholders see it as an option to avoid paying in full—and many often do not. If you feel that you can be self-disciplined in paying the total amount each month, go ahead and use your card for those regular purchases. If you feel that you will not be able to control your spending habits, or if after the first statement arrives you find that you are unable to pay in full, it is recommended that you stay away from trying to accumulate points in the first place. Credit cards offer these points and benefits as incentives to use your credit card. Generally, many consumers then begin to use their credit cards more frequently, increase their balances, and pay more interest, which is the intention of the credit card issuers! So you need to be very careful in such situations.

For those who find a credit card convenient, who feel it provides a sense of security or even offers rewarding benefits, a credit card can truly shine like gold. For those, however, who have seen the fool's gold of credit cards, the cards are little more than pieces of plastic. So what type of credit card is right for you? Our next section, "Eenie, Meanie, Miney, Moe," should help answer that question.

Paying Uncle Sam with your credit card? Putting the down payment for your next home on a credit card? Sound like a dream? These dreams are soon to become reality as credit card companies expand into the growing number of money-making opportunities.

EENIE, MEANIE, MINEY, MOE

What credit card is right for you? That depends on how you plan to use it and the type of individual you are.

If you've read this far, you are by now on your way out of credit card debt. It's a good time to consider exactly which credit card perfectly suits your needs if you choose to continue to use one. The following sections discuss the different types of credit cards that can be found in our society.

For Those Who Pay in Full

> *"Freeloader," in terms of financial lending, is a consumer who doesn't pay interest because he always pays off his balance due on time . . .*
> —CONSUMER REPORTS

If you plan to pay your credit card on time, every month, you will want a credit card with no annual fee and a long grace period. Interest rates will not be important, since they apply only to credit cards that carry a balance. But always be careful; perhaps in the past you thought you'd be paying every month in full and you haven't. It's an unfortunate trap that some of our characters have fallen into—especially Jennifer, who thought her new job would cover her expenses, but her love for shoes made that impossible.

For Those Who Carry a Balance

If you do plan to carry a balance (you know that you will not be able to pay in full each month), the most important factor to take into consideration is the interest rate, or APR.

Even if an annual fee seems high, the low standard interest rate will more than compensate. And if the interest rate is temporary, you will be able to make it more permanent once you utilize the skills you've received from this book.

One of the major factors that hindered the Joneses' and Bob's credit card debt from decreasing was the interest rates on their credit cards. If they had credit cards with low interest rates in the first place, they would not be where they are now.

For Those Who Can't Get a Credit Card

For those who can't get a credit card, there are "secured" cards, which are unlike regular credit cards (otherwise known as "unsecured" cards). To qualify for a secured card you must maintain a savings account with the card's issuer. The credit line is usually 50% to 100% of the amount in the savings account. Keep in mind that secured cards tend to have higher interest rates and higher annual fees than unsecured cards. Also, because more banks are offering secured cards than ever before, make sure to shop around for a savings account with a decent interest rate. Some banks do not even give you interest on your deposit!

A secured card can really help your credit report, especially if you have a bad credit history or no credit history at all. Just make sure that the credit card issuer reports your credit card transactions to the credit bureau.

For Those Who Are Very Responsible

Next, there are the "charge" cards, such as American Express and Diners Club. Unlike unsecured credit cards, payments for these cards must be made in full each month and there is no interest. These cards should be used only by responsible individuals. This is especially true with American Express, for which there is no predetermined spending limit. It is very easy to spend more than what one can truly afford, and many individuals end up transferring American Express balances to other credit cards.* If used properly and responsibly, charge cards can be very useful, especially with the benefits some have to offer. One last thing to remember is that charge cards generally carry high annual fees.

For Those Who Want a Limited Card

Retail cards such as credit cards issued by department stores and oil companies are a restricted type of credit card, in that they can be used only in connection with the companies that issued them. Higher interest rates are tied in with retail cards, and their approval rate for credit applications is higher than that for regular credit cards. All in all, these cards are useless. Unless there is a retail card that offers some sort of benefit that might be of great use, or you are trying to build up your credit history, avoid these credit cards.

For Those Who Want to Avoid Debt

Somewhat new in the credit card industry are debit cards. Debit cards imitate credit cards in that you can use them wherever credit cards are accepted. Similar to secured credit cards because they are linked to a bank account, they are unlike any other credit card in that there is no interest

---

*As we all know, the interest applied by credit cards is a very large source of revenue. This has also caught the eye of charge card issuers. American Express offers its card members the option to pay for large purchases over time. Whether it is because many card members have been transferring their balances or charge cards simply want more revenue, card members now have the option to pay over time—just another trap to avoid.

charged and the amount due is always deducted directly from your checking account, as if you'd written a personal check.* These cards actually discourage the consumer from spending what he or she doesn't have. So although they do not build your credit history, as a credit card would, they certainly can keep you from getting into too much debt in a way a credit card never would!

A debit card is ideal for Tom and Jennifer, for it will limit their spending habits and in turn save them from future financial troubles, but it will not build up their credit history as would a credit card. The Joneses and Bob will certainly benefit from using a debit card to avoid accumulating additional credit card debt.

Once you have found a suitable type of credit card, you also need to make sure it will complement your lifestyle. Make sure a particular card has a large enough credit limit to match your spending habits (which you should not even think of doing until your debt is at *no more* than 10% of your monthly income) or a credit limit that allows for transfers of your other balances.** The card should be accepted by the majority of today's merchants. And, of course, there should also be enhancements and services that appeal to you: travel insurance or points for free purchases.

For the most recent information on the best credit cards to choose in terms of interest rates, annual fees, grace periods, and other benefits, make sure to visit my Internet website at www.creditcardfreedom.com. For further details, see "The Adventure Continues Online," on page 176.

---

*Some banks charge fees per debit card transaction that can be as high as $1.50, while other banks charge a monthly fee that can be as high as $5.

**If a large credit limit is what landed you in debt in the first place, and you don't want to cancel the card once you are out of debt (so you can use it to cover an unexpected emergency), contact the issuer and ask to have your limit significantly decreased—$2,000 is sufficient for most unexpected emergencies. This will deter future temptations.

You should be aware that depending on the amount of debt in your current open accounts, it might be difficult to receive the credit card of your choice. A word of caution: If you apply for one or two credit cards and you are rejected for having too many card balances already, or because the amounts owed on your accounts are too high, wait until those amounts decrease significantly before applying again. Also, do not apply for too many credit cards (three or more) or other types of loans at one time, because each inquiry will be noted on your credit report. Too many inquiries will give lenders the impression that an applicant is desperate for a loan, and on that basis alone they would most likely reject the application.

> *Seven of the most common words or phrases used in credit card advertising: low, enjoy, save (savings), free, no fee, pre-approved, apply.*

Remember, the difference between choosing the right credit card or the wrong one can mean the difference between being free of credit card debt and being captured by it. The war against credit card debt is best won by those consumers who pay close attention to the terms and conditions of any type of credit card—secured, debit, or unsecured.

After knowing these important concluding facts, you're probably curious how credit card issuers finally determine whether to issue you a card or not. The next section, "How You Compare to the Joneses," should give you a good idea.

HOW YOU COMPARE TO THE JONESES

After completing numerous credit card applications, **Jennifer**, the **Joneses**, and **Bob** know quite well where they *stand in terms of the issuer's eye. **Tom**, however, lacks a significant number of credit cards, and because of that he also lacks the knowledge of how he is viewed by credit card issuers, which might just surprise him!*

In life, we always seem to be tested on our qualifications, whether in school or in comparing ourselves to the next-door neighbors, the Joneses. Credit cards are no exception. Credit card issuers like to see how we compare to others; how much of a risk, if any, we are to them; and most important, if they'll make a profit from us.

The comparison method used is a type of credit scoring system in which every aspect of our lives is graded on a point system. Credit card issuers will award points for specific factors they feel are significant. For example, they will review your credit history, your income, your outstanding debt, whether you own a home or a car, how many dependents you have, how many years you have been at your current job, and even how old you are. If you make $30,000 a year, you might be awarded ten points. But if you make $20,000 a year, you might be awarded only five points. Eventually, all points are added up, and those people with the most points are considered the least risky and subsequently the most desirable cardholders. The issuers will, of course, review your credit history, which generally has the strongest influence on the final approval. An individual might have $200,000 in liquid assets, but if he or she has a poor credit history, or even no credit history, the individual will have a hard time being approved by a lender.

NO INCOME? NO CREDIT HISTORY? NO PROBLEM!

So much has changed in the past decade. Credit card issuers no longer aim solely toward high-income individuals with excellent credit histories. Because credit card companies make the majority of their money through interest rates, and because most high-income individuals pay their balances in full every month, the companies have now been aiming toward higher risk individuals, such as low-wage workers and those with less-than-perfect credit reports. Even college students, many of whom have been consistently avoided, now receive a record number of credit cards. This has caused controversy for educational boards and parents (especially because they are paying the bills), since many students are getting into debt without having any significant income (see "The College Students," on page 122). Higher risk individuals, those with low incomes, usually carry a month-to-month balance at a higher interest rate—profit in the eyes of the credit card companies. There are always some consumers who are unable to make payments, but the issuers' profits far exceed their losses simply because of the high interest rates consumers are charged.

Unfortunately, even if you are denied credit, you will not have access to a company's credit scoring system. By law, however, you're entitled to know why you've been denied credit: It could be lack of income, outstanding debt, or numerous other factors. By knowing why you were denied credit, you will be able to ascertain what needs to be done before you apply for the next credit card or loan.

Sometimes, the credit bureau that provided your credit history to the credit card issuer has incorrect information, and by law you are entitled to receive the same report within sixty days of being denied a credit card. These rules also apply for other types of loans, such as mortgages, equity loans, and car loans. For further information on receiving credit reports, see "Checking Your Credit History," on page 154.

Credit card issuers usually try to minimize risk and maximize profits by finding the right consumer—the ideal "Tom" or "Jennifer." But sometimes not all goes as planned, and to minimize losses, credit card companies simply expand their realm of profit making, which is explained in our next section, "A Very Profitable Business."

THE COLLEGE STUDENTS

Credit card issuers are now finding that college students are very profitable risks. When students apply, they are not screened the same way other applicants are. Even though the applications ask specific information, the only true qualification is that the individual be a student at a university or college. Credit card issuers know that the student market is profitable simply because of the insurance the students carry: their parents' income. Also, the majority of students continue to use their credit cards after they graduate and throughout their lives—an added bonus.

Students are lured into getting credit cards for the freedom they offer, but do they really offer such freedom? Incentives are even given to students, such as free gifts—T-shirts or baseball caps—if only they complete an application.

Those individuals and groups—such as parents and educational boards—who feel manipulating students is wrong are retaliating by informing students of credit card evils through classes and college newspapers. The states of Massachusetts and New York are even considering banning any type of promotion for credit cards on campus. Credit cards can be very useful to students if they know how to manage them. Many students, however, are not fully acquainted with managing personal finances.

A 1996 survey from the Phoenix Home Life Mutual Insurance Company found that 60% of college stu-

> dents have a credit card for personal use, 60% of
> those having cards pay their balance in full for each
> billing cycle, 33% comprehend the word budget, and
> only 20% comprehend "buying on credit." Knowing
> the results of this survey, it is no wonder the credit
> card issuers make huge profits from students.

A VERY PROFITABLE BUSINESS

Because of their long-time experiences with credit cards, the **Joneses** *and* **Bob** *are probably very familiar with the profits involved in the credit card business.* **Tom** *and* **Jennifer,** *however, might not be aware that there is more to a credit card than meets the eye.*

If you think that credit card companies make money through charging interest only, think again. It is true that applying interest results in the largest profit, but that is not the only method of revenue. As in any business, expansion and diversity are often the keys to success, and credit card companies have most definitely not ignored them. Following are other sources of revenue into which credit card issuers have been successfully able to expand.

MEMBERSHIP DOESN'T HAVE ITS PRIVILEGES

Even though every credit card does not have an annual fee, and more and more credit card issuers are reducing their annual fees, there are still many that do have such fees. You might not think $20 is much to pay, but multiply that figure by 250,000 card holders. That would equal $5 million a year for one credit card. Many credit card issuers offer more than one type of credit card—sometimes just to be able to offer at least one credit card with an annual fee—to obtain the extra revenue. So don't be surprised when a credit card offers a low interest rate; it is likely to be accompanied by an annual fee.

WHEN YOU MISBEHAVE

Transaction fees such as late payment fees, cash advance fees, over-the-credit-limit fees, returned check fees, and stop payment fees are just a few of the ways credit card companies enjoy making money. Imagine that half of the cardholders were charged $30—as one of the fees just mentioned—and, as before, there were 250,000 members. Multiply 125,000 by $30, for a total of $3.75 million. Not bad for a mistake a consumer might make. Now perhaps you can see more clearly why credit cards charge fees: to keep card members in order, to cover their own costs (which are minimal), and to increase their revenue.

HAVE EVERYONE CHIP IN

Did you know that whenever a purchase or service is acquired through your credit card, a percentage of the amount of that purchase or service (usually between 2% and 5%) is also paid by the merchant? As you might imagine, merchants do not like this idea, but they know that many customers will only make a purchase with a credit card, especially if the purchase is expensive. The credit card, then, acts as a middle man, making money from the buyer and also from the seller.

SHOP IN YOUR SLIPPERS

Many credit card issuers offer products through catalogs. Usually, the products can be paid for with a monthly payment plan, or even sometimes by points that accumulate through the use of the credit card. However, the prices of the products are generally high compared to similar items on sale at a nearby retailer. Though the convenience of looking through the catalog and being able to pay in installments is very inviting, it ultimately traps many consumers into payment plans accompanied by high interest rates. It is also a wonderful way of reaping additional profits for the credit card issuers.

ADVERTISING HAS NO LIMITS

Ever notice special products or services offered through your credit card? Outside companies often advertise through your credit card's monthly statement. Whether the product is a trip to Hawaii or a calculator clock, more and more companies are finding it worthwhile to advertise with credit cards because of the growing number of credit cardholders. Whether or not the cardholder chooses to buy the offered merchandise or service, the credit card issuer makes money. Even if the merchandise is not purchased, the credit card issuer has made a profit by selling the advertising space for the product, and if there is a purchase, the credit card issuer benefits from a percentage of the revenue (as was just explained in "Have Everyone Chip In"), since the cardholder would have to use the credit card to make the purchase.

Nothing Is Free

Sometimes credit cards offer free trials of specific products or services—such as credit report monitoring and magazine subscriptions—that can be ordered for thirty days or for several months. These services are great for credit card companies, because many consumers either forget or do not want to bother with the hassle of canceling the service, which usually must be done within a specified cancellation period. This, in turn, brings easy extra revenue to the credit card company.

> *And what about those "free gifts" offered with more than suspiciously high shipping and handling charges? For example, those "free" twenty-minute calling cards actually cost $3.95 for activation, shipping, and handling. If you do the math, those "free" calling cards cost you nearly twenty cents per minute to use. But some consumers still accept that these are free gifts.*

So there you have it, all the tricks that make credit cards a very profitable business, at least for those companies that are managed properly. Even those individuals who pay their bills on time and in full every month might still benefit the credit card issuer.* And although they've been able to make money from all types of credit card holders and transactions, it will always remain true that credit card issuers still make the most money through charging interest rates.

*Revenue Distribution for Credit Card Issuers***

- 76% from finance charges
- 11% from fees paid by merchants
- 4% from late fees
- 4% from cash advance charges
- 5% from annual and other charges

---

*Be aware that some companies can charge you a fee if you pay your balance in full each month, but don't be too preoccupied, as it has yet to become trendy in the credit card industry.

**Henry Capell, *Business Week*, September 23, 1996.

If you still have doubts, take a look at the Joneses as an example: They paid over $8,000 in interest last year alone, which breaks down to over $667 for each credit card—not bad for a piece of plastic. But the Joneses are not alone, as the next section explains.

CREDIT CARD—FACTS OR THEORIES?

*This section will interest **Bob** more than the others because of his interest in finances and statistics. But after reading this section, you will have learned even more: that if you have credit card debt, you are not alone!*

> Definition of a credit card: a misconception of money, a misinterpretation of freedom, and a misjudgment of responsibility for those who use them.

Fact: Since the introduction of the credit card in the 1950s, credit card debt has reached an all-time high among American consumers. That's good news for credit card issuers and those who write books like this one, but bad news for the consumer.

For example, did you know that the average American family has over $7,000 in credit card debt? For the first time, consumer debt has surpassed the $1 trillion mark. And of this amount, $450 billion reflects that of credit card debt.

So how is it possible to have such a large figure? The fact of the matter is, there are millions of U.S. consumers who have access to credit cards; in fact, there are enough credit cards in the United States to match the population of 260 million.

And the trouble doesn't stop at the record credit card debt

level. Late payments for credit cards have hit a new high of 3.72% for the total number of cards in 1996, and delinquencies have reached a record high of 5.45% in 1996 alone, based on dollars of credit in outstanding balances.*

At the same time, there's also been a large increase in filing for bankruptcy, over 1.17 million claims in 1996, up 27% from 1995.** (However, a study from the Federal Reserve found these figures to be unrealistic, mainly because the percentage of increase in personal bankruptcies was due to the large number of baby boomers borrowing and not to rising credit card debt levels. The Fed argues that the share of baby boomers filing for personal bankruptcy does not significantly differ from that of past generations because the fact of the matter is, there are more of them.[+]

Although the economy is currently doing well, especially with all this consumer spending, there will be a point at which people will need to pay their debts and subsequently not spend as much, which in turn could provide some important danger signals.

The current $450 billion credit card debt, however, is hard to analyze (most credit card issuers claim that figure is exaggerated in the first place), simply because it does not necessarily reflect that U.S. consumers have that much in revolving credit card debt. For example, some (approximately 36% of all credit card users[++]) pay off their balances in full each month, so not all of the $450 billion incurs monthly interest. But because of the rapid growth of credit card usage in the United States, one thing is certain—we are at an all-time high in credit card debt, whether revolving or not.

Investors Business Daily, March 3, 1997.

**Business Week*, April 28, 1997.

[+]*Investors Business Daily*, August 22, 1997.

[++]*Business Week*, September 23, 1996.

But who is to blame, the consumer, because of ignorance and uncontrollable spending habits (Jennifer), or the credit card issuers, because of tricky advertising and mail offers with temporary low interest rates (the Joneses and their accumulated debt because of expiring teaser rates)? Both sides would surely have their arguments. If credit cards had never been invented and people instead used debit cards, consumers might not have accumulated debt beyond their means. But who really knows where, or how, consumers might have done their spending and what other type of debt would have increased?

So what does the future have in store for credit cards, at least in terms of remaining a profitable business? Whether because of an increase in delinquencies or an increase toward marketing to higher risk individuals, as in any business, if market conditions change, sometimes adjustments to the business need to be made. Therefore, to reduce losses, many credit card companies are increasing their fees for delinquencies and over-the-limit balances; they are also lowering minimum payment configurations. For example, the minimum payment requirement might be lowered from $1/48$ to $1/50$ of a balance, which, while increasing finance charges in the long run, will lower the monthly minimum payment due, in turn helping those who are in financial trouble stay in good standing with their credit cards.

A 1997 survey by the Federal Reserve showed that credit card issuers have been making adjustments, at least in terms of credit card applications. The survey showed that fewer than 25% of American banks have tightened their standards and that 25% had lowered the amount that consumers could borrow from their credit cards.* Even though these adjustments are occurring at a slow pace, they're reducing losses associated with higher risk individuals and

Investors Business Daily, August 25, 1997.

are ensuring continued profitability for the credit card issuers. But whether these adjustments are for the long term or the short term is anyone's guess.

After reading this short statistics section, you should feel relieved, knowing that you are not alone in credit card debt, but not encouraged to continue spending on your credit cards, since you now know so much of America is in credit card debt!

You've read this far and should be pleased with the results you have so far achieved in lowering and reducing the burden imposed by your credit cards. You might also now consider yourself a credit card expert, knowing everything from the tricks credit card companies use and how to avoid them to the national credit card debt figure and why credit cards are such a profitable business.

Still, there is more to know. You might want to be prepared if some unexpected expense were to arise, for example. The following chapter, "What You *Might* Want to Know," offers some alternative ways to handle your credit card debt.

What You *Might* Want to Know

CUT THOSE EXPENSES

*Budgeting is always a good idea. It would be most beneficial for the **Joneses** to do so, since they have so many financial responsibilities. **Jennifer** will also benefit as her responsibilities increase over time, and **Tom** will gain some useful knowledge that he can apply in the future. **Bob**, on the other hand, doesn't need to budget as much as he needs to organize his personal finances.*

After becoming organized and coming to terms with your debt, it is important to budget your lifestyle. It will be more difficult than it already is to get out of debt if you are continuously making unnecessary purchases every month. Many individuals who have large credit card balances often think that since their balances are already so large an additional purchase will not make a difference, which is a misconception Jennifer has as she continues to buy more shoes! Thoughts like this only result in more debt, whether it's $25 or $500!

It will be hard at first to stop using your credit cards, but the temptation to do so will decrease as time passes and you use them less. Remember, saving money can be thought of as making money! I've mentioned numerous times that you should not cancel your credit cards, and perhaps by not canceling them it becomes even harder not to use them, so I recommend that you take those cards out of your purse or wallet and place them somewhere in your home that will not allow you easy access, such as in a locked box you keep in the attic. It is often the easy access of reaching for the credit card that causes many individuals to get into high credit card debt in the first place.

LIFE'S BUT A BUDGET

Take a look at your monthly expenses. Where has your income been going? The most difficult part of budgeting is seeing where your money is actually going, especially if you use a lot of cash. It will help if you organize your expenses as you did when organizing your credit cards. First, it is recommended that you keep all receipts, especially for purchases made by cash, so that at the end of the month you can put some time aside and analyze your expenses. Just take a look at the following budget sample representing some of Jennifer's expenses.

BUDGET SAMPLE

	Sept. 98	*Oct. 98*	*Nov. 98*	*Dec. 98*
Rent	$ 500.00	$ 500.00	$ 500.00	$ 500.00
Food	$ 300.00	$ 275.00	$ 250.00	$ 240.00
Utilities	$ 350.00	$ 200.00	$ 150.00	$ 120.00
Credit Cards	$ 150.00	$ 150.00	$ 150.00	$ 150.00
Car—Parking	$ 100.00	$ 40.00	$ 40.00	$ 40.00

	Sept. 98	*Oct. 98*	*Nov. 98*	*Dec. 98*
Car—Gas	$ 75.00	$ 40.00	$ 30.00	$ 40.00
Entertainment	$ 200.00	$ 70.00	$ 50.00	$ 30.00
Total:	$1,675.00	$1,275.00	$1,170.00	$1,120.00

There will always be expenses that will be difficult, if not impossible, to lower—Jennifer's rent, for example. She could move to another home with lower rent, but that might be difficult and inconvenient, and the trouble of relocating might not be worth the few dollars that might be saved. But what about her utility bills? By conserving electricity, heat, and even making fewer phone calls, she could save considerably. Then there's parking. How about if she used public transportation? She would also save on gasoline and other car-related expenses. You're probably getting the picture: Cut expenses that are within normal means that do not drastically alter your lifestyle.

Any money saved should go toward your credit card debt, because it will obviously help reduce your debt in the long run. As one can see in Jennifer's case, after doing a little saving in just one month, she would have an additional $400 to her credit card debt within her first month of budgeting.

For your convenience, I have supplied two charts at the end of this section. One has a list of general expenses and the other is a blank chart for you to list your own personal expenses. As you did with your credit cards, you will need to analyze your expenses and find out which expenses you can reduce without causing too much inconvenience to your lifestyle. Just remember: "Organize, Analyze, and Reduce!" are the keys to your financial freedom.

Those who are consistently overwhelmed by monthly payments to their credit cards sometimes find that stretching out payments over a longer period of time can ease the financial burden. So if you find that budgeting is not a possible alternative, or does not offer a significant movement of funds toward your credit card debt, then consider consolidating your debt, which is explained in the next section.

It's amazing how much plastic can cost you these days.

—A CREDIT CARD CONSUMER

THE BUDGET CHART

Monthly Expenses									
Living									
Rent									
Food									
Utilities									
Telephone									
Electric									
Water									
Gas									
Loans									
Credit Card(s)									
Mortgage(s)									
Car(s)									
Student Loan(s)									
Insurance									
Health									
Property									

THE BUDGET CHART (continued)

Monthly Expenses								
Car								
Insurance								
Gas								
Maintanence								
Education								
Tuition								
Room and Board								
Supplies								
Additional								
Clothing								
Transportation								
Entertainment								
Vacation								
Health and Beauty								
Other								
Total:								

THE BUDGET CHART

Monthly Expenses

Total:

THE BUDGET CHART (continued)

Monthly Expenses

Total:

CONSOLIDATING YOUR DEBT

*By consolidating debts, the **Joneses** could lower their monthly obligations and **Bob**'s lack of organization could be solved.*

So you have done everything you can to lower the cost of your debt and are now living on a very tight budget. But you are unable to increase your income, and the burden of all the payments is becoming overwhelming. This is the moment when you might want to consider consolidating your debt, perhaps at least as an alternative plan if an unexpected expense were to come up.

The Joneses have considered consolidating their debt as a backup. If, for some reason, their monthly income should decrease, consolidation would reduce their monthly obligations from $900 to $400 of their $45,127.32 credit card debt.

Consolidation is as simple as combining all your debt into one easy payment per month, sometimes at a lower interest rate than your previous debts. Consolidating your debt can be done with equity loans, equity lines of credit, second mortgages, and other strategies. We'll now weigh the good, and the negative, aspects of consolidation.

THE GOOD PART

- ✀ You will be relieved of the many payments you must make regularly.
- ✀ Depending on the consolidated loan's terms and duration, your monthly payments can be reduced by half, or even more.
- ✀ The interest on the loan might be tax deductible.
- ✀ You will not have to worry about late payments, missing payments, transaction fees, and other penalties.

✂ You will have less paperwork, such as writing checks and keeping up with all your balances.

✂ Your credit report will prosper because you will have reduced all the credit card accounts into one large account. (Furthermore, many financial institutions consider credit card debt as "bad" debt. So by consolidating, you are turning bad debt into good debt.)

✂ The introductory interest rate might be discounted for the first six to twelve months. In turn, this might be lower than the average interest rate that applied to your original total credit card debt.

THE NOT-SO-GOOD PART

✂ The lender might have certain requirements, such as sufficient income, a clean credit report, and significant collateral. Such factors will be reviewed before any approval of a consolidation loan.

✂ There might be some fees added to the loan that, in turn, will increase your overall debt if you are unable to pay them up front.

✂ If you have a fifteen- to thirty-year-long-term loan, your monthly payments will be reduced, but you will end up paying more in finance charges. If the introductory rate expires, you might end up with a higher interest rate.

✂ By consolidating your debt, you are turning unsecured debt into secured debt. In other words, your debt will involve your assets, and if you do not pay your consolidation loan you risk losing some, if not all, of your assets. Because credit cards are unsecured debt, there is no involvement of your assets.

✂ Even though consolidating your debt will most likely result in a loan with a low rate, the credit cards themselves can actually offer a lower average interest rate. Nevertheless, you need to put aside a little time to manage your credit cards; either consolidate for a continuous low interest rate or take a chance with the credit cards for an even lower rate.

Remember that consolidating your debt works only if you close your credit card accounts. If you do not, you might go back to using your credit cards and will be in worse shape than before. However, most issuers of consolidating loans require that you close certain—if not all—credit card accounts at the contract signing.

You need to decide what is best for you. If you feel you need to reduce your monthly expenses temporarily and think that in the near future you will be able to pay off more of your loan, in turn avoiding future interest charges, then consolidation would be a good idea. Make absolutely sure there are no prepayment penalties (some banks charge a penalty fee if the loan is paid in advance) toward the loan.

It is best to shop around when considering loan consolidation for your outstanding debt; go to your local bank or review ads in your local newspaper. Since there are numerous types of loans with different interest rates and terms, it is best to find the type of loan that most easily suits your needs and capabilities. Generally speaking, the larger national banks will usually offer lower rates and fewer transaction fees than a local bank. Make sure you understand every term and agreement before signing any contract. The loan representative should be able to answer all your questions; if not, you might want to consider going to another lender. For a list of low interest rate loans with no transaction fees, visit my Internet web site at www.creditcard-freedom.com.

Unfortunately, for whatever reason, not everyone who applies for a consolidating loan gets approved. If this happens to you, do not despair, for as we move into the following section, readers are offered a variety of choices and possibilities for winning the war against their credit card debt.

UNIQUE OPTIONS

There are several alternative methods designed to help attack your credit card debt. This section should provide you with at least one that is perfect for you!

If you are still feeling stuck and unable to handle your credit card debt, read on, for there are still other ways to lessen the burden. Some of the following suggestions might not be viable alternatives for all individuals, but you might be surprised as to what you *can* do!

A SECOND JOB

Your first option is to increase your income by getting a second job and using that income to help reduce your credit card debt. This is—obviously—one of the best ways to pay off the debt. Unfortunately, working a second job, even if only part-time, might be difficult for some and impossible for others.

The job option is a great opportunity for Tom, since one thing he has is free time. By finding a simple part-time job he could really cut down his debt.

YOUR ASSETS

You might want to consider selling any assets you might have—jewelry, cars, even a house—for each contribution to lowering your debt will greatly help you in the long run. However, you must always be careful in terms of selling any investments that might be providing a large return. It is best to get professional advice when selling one's investments in order to pay off debt.

Depending on your situation, part, rather than all, of an investment might be sold to lessen the burden of your debt. It depends on the amount of credit card debt you are carrying and the average interest rate you are paying.

If you are paying an average interest rate of 18% on your credit cards, you would require an investment offering a return *equal* to or *greater than* 18% to prevent you from selling that investment. However, if the average interest rate on your credit cards is around 6% (which it should be after following the advice in this book), it would not be worthwhile to sell an asset that is providing an 18% annual return. Always make sure to thoroughly analyze your assets and their annual returns before making any final decisions.

A Telephone Call

Another option is to contact the credit card issuers and explain the situation you are in. Be honest and straightforward with them; you will be surprised to find that most will be willing to work out a special payment plan since the last thing a credit card issuer wants you to do is not pay at all. It would be a good idea when you are negotiating payments, however, to ask how they will be reporting the circumstances of the payments to the credit bureau, for you do not want a negative mark on your credit report.

Also, do not wait for them to call *you*, or wait until the outstanding debt has been taken over by a collection agency, simply because you will have less negotiating power in such situations.

How long you've had the credit card and your payment history with the credit card issuer are vital here. Therefore, the Joneses and Bob have the option to consider it.

PROFESSIONAL HELP

Need an extra hand? Think about trying a counseling service for debt management. There are several, easily found in your local yellow pages. Start with a well-established service. Often these services will negotiate with the credit card issuer to lower your interest rates and even lower your minimum payments. Although counseling services are in the business to help you handle your debt, most of the services they offer you can do yourself. Too many individuals, however, are simply too overburdened with debt and don't have a lot of time, and for them paying the counseling service fee might be worthwhile.

Be advised that some of these companies charge very high fees, so make sure to investigate several services before accepting any help, and always be suspicious about those companies that seem to guarantee the impossible, such as promising you will be "Debt Free in 90 Days."

Not sure where to start? You can take your first step and contact one of the following services.

Credit Counseling Services

- ✂ The National Foundation for Consumer Credit: A nonprofit organization located throughout the United States that will help you reorganize your outstanding debt and payments to creditors; 301-589-5600. (You can call their toll-free number, 800-388-2227, for a credit counseling service in your area, or visit their web site at www.nfcc.org.)

- ✂ Consumer Credit Counseling Services (CCCS): Services are generally free, or, depending on your situation, there might be a small monthly fee for handling your debt and negotiating with creditors; 800-577-2227.

If the Joneses and Bob find that time is not on their side, they might choose the option of turning to a counseling service. And even though there might be a fee, it will be a minimum cost in relation to the large finance charges that would otherwise accumulate on their credit cards.

CREDIT CARD SURFING

This final option applies only to those who are in temporary financial trouble. By temporary, I mean a few months. Remember those special offer checks you used to transfer balances to cards with lower rates? Those transfer checks can also be used instead of paying minimum due amounts.

In tight financial situations there is a way to avoid payments and do transfers between balances. For example, if you have three credit cards, one with a balance of $2,000 and the others without balances, you can transfer the $2,000 between accounts. It can be done as long as there are sufficient credit limits and you have balance transfer checks. By doing this and timing the transfers properly, you can avoid paying anything for three months or more.*

Remember that this recommendation is only for those who are in serious temporary financial trouble; because no payments are going toward your debt at that time and interest is being applied, your credit card debt will increase (especially if there are transaction fees for every transfer that is made). Obviously, it's not a situation that can go on

---

*Earlier, it was stated that you should always send your payment as soon as you receive a statement, especially when transferring to a lower interest rate. In terms of credit card surfing, you want to wait as long as possible before reaching the due payment date. The reason for this is simple: You might be able to miss the closing date of the credit card you are transferring to. For example, if the closing date is the fifteenth of September but the credit card issuer receives the transferred balance on the sixteenth, it will not appear until the October billing statement. This gives you two billing cycles instead of one to make another transfer and avoid any payments.

forever, since you have a limited credit limit. It also might result negatively in your payment history regarding a particular credit card, as you never actually made payments, only transfers.*

If you choose the credit card surfing method to help out in a tight financial situation, it usually helps to have several credit cards and a high flexibility rating (see "Your Flexibility," on page 45). As you probably recall, your flexibility rating determines your ability to move balances around. The Joneses—even though they have twelve credit cards—have a very low flexibility rating of 1.08, which makes credit card surfing very difficult. Bob and Jennifer also have low flexibility ratings of 1.78 and 1.55, respectively, but would be in a better position in delaying their payments than the Joneses. On the other hand, even though Tom has only two credit cards, he has a very high flexibility rating of 3.13, giving him the opportunity, if called for, to move balances back and forth.

ADDITIONAL HELP

Another alternative for those who are in serious debt is to contact Debtors Anonymous, which is a national organization designed to help those who cannot control their spending habits and consequently often increase their debt. If you feel you have a problem that requires more help than anything recommended in this book, it might be a good idea to contact Debtors Anonymous at the following address: Debtors Anonymous, General Service Board, P.O. Box 400, Grand Central Station, New York, NY 10016.

By now, many of you have found additional sources, or

---

*Some credit card issuers are able to track when an actual payment was made and when it was a balance transfer check from another credit card issuer. The tracking is used so the lender has a better understanding of how the consumer uses the credit card.

techniques, to help you reduce your credit card debt. Not surprisingly, a few readers might not yet have found a way to finally defeat their credit card debt. For those individuals there is one final possibility—a strategic move that one in every hundred households made in 1997—and chances are you've heard about it: filing for bankruptcy.

Further details are explained in the next section, "The Last Alternative."

THE LAST ALTERNATIVE

*Because they're young, have time to build a positive credit history, and lack sufficient credit card debt, **Tom** and **Jennifer** would not be good candidates for bankruptcy. **Bob** has too many assets and his income is too high, so the only ones who might qualify and benefit if things truly go bad would be the **Joneses**, because of their overwhelming financial responsibilities.*

> *Get them while they last! Congress might tighten bankruptcy rules as filings are reaching all-time highs. According to credit card issuers, the process might be just too easy.*

Because of the increasing amount of credit card debt, it's no surprise that there's been an increase in bankruptcy claims. Filing for bankruptcy is like getting a second chance. It is generally accepted that if your debt is over 50% of your current income, bankruptcy would be a good choice. There are many types of bankruptcies to file for. In terms of credit cards, you would chose Bankruptcy Chapter 7, which deals with unsecured debt. (Unsecured debt refers to debt that is not tied to property or collateral that can be seized, or repossessed, if the debt is not paid. Credit cards, fortunately, are considered unsecured debt.) You might also file under Chapter 13, which does not completely wipe out your debt but instead lowers your monthly payment obligations. Even though lenders receive a smaller monthly payment, they obviously prefer Chapter 13 to Chapter 7.

Filing for bankruptcy takes three to six months, much paperwork, time, and usually a lawyer. In fact, an attorney is highly recommended if you are unfamiliar with the process, terms, and conditions of filing for bankruptcy.

Generally speaking, those who file for bankruptcy have experienced a sudden change in lifestyle, such as divorce or the loss of a job. Under such circumstances, and without additional sources of income or assets, many turn toward bankruptcy as a last resort, which it truly is, since it will seriously affect your credit history for seven to ten years and you cannot file again within six years. Also, not all your debts might be cleared, and you might be required to give up personal assets, depending on how the judge determines your financial standing and future capabilities.

If you cosign a credit card application, be aware that you might be held liable if the primary holder defaults on the account or even claims bankruptcy. No matter what your relationship to the primary holder, credit card issuers will seek payment wherever they legally can.

Fortunately, by taking control of their credit card debt at an early stage, the Joneses have significantly reduced the odds of needing to file for bankruptcy in the near future.

So unless all else fails, stay away from filing for bankruptcy!

Referrals

✂ American Bankruptcy Board of Certification: Offers referrals of attorneys nearest to your location who handle bankruptcy cases. These attorneys are certified by the American Bankruptcy Board; 703-739-1023.

Now that we have introduced the many alternative methods that provide ammunition in the battle against your credit card debt, we move on to a completely different subject, one that will bring you to "Your Final Destination," starting with how important it is to be a responsible and wise cardholder.

Part Three

Your Final Destination

Better Safe . . . Than Sorry

You have successfully completed Part One and Part Two of *Credit Card Debt . . .* and have applied numerous methods and strategies toward defeating your credit card debt. There are still a few more suggestions and guidelines to help polish your new knowledge in credit card debt management. The following chapters will now show you the road to becoming a wiser and more responsible credit card holder.

CREDIT REPAIR AGENCIES

No matter what type of individual you are or what kind of trouble you are in, you want to stay away from these folks!

If it's not the credit card companies trying to take advantage of your credit card debt, it's someone else: the credit repair agency. Otherwise known as "credit doctors," they are supposed to clean up and fix any negative information on your credit report.

They will claim to be able to perform nearly impossible tasks to make your credit report spotless. In reality, however, they cannot get rid of negative information that is correct, so, in fact, you do not need them. Maybe some minor adjustments can be made, but whatever they can do, so can you. Paying for their services, then, is like throwing money away, especially because many require you to pay up front, and what you end up with is no significant change in your credit report. Some even claim they'll be able to change your identity! Be advised that if any illegal actions are ever taken by the credit doctors, *you* can be held liable for the consequences.

Although they might sound appealing, you really *don't* need a credit repair agency, since you can easily call up your credit bureau for a report and check any negative information for yourself. Credit bureaus are discussed at length in the next section.

CHECKING YOUR CREDIT HISTORY

*This section is useful for everyone. For **Tom**, it would be an educational experience since he has yet to build up a credit history; **Jennifer** might spend a little less knowing what might happen if she can't pay her debts; the **Joneses** could benefit greatly to make sure everything is being reported properly; and **Bob**, though he's checked his credit history before, will not be hurt by checking again.*

If you are managing quite a few credit cards, it might be a good idea to make sure your credit history is up-to-date and in good standing (that is, if you have been making your payments on time) every eight to twelve months. Your credit history is very important, and with millions of transactions being made each day, mistakes do happen; in fact, the more credit cards you have, the more likely a mistake can occur. That is why the Joneses, who have twelve credit cards, should check their credit history more frequently than Tom, who has only two.

Did you know that credit history reports are no longer requested only by lenders but are also subject to the prying eyes of prospective employers (only with your written permission, of course)? Yet another reason to keep your credit history in good standing.

If you do notice a mistake—large or small—on your credit report you should contact the credit bureau immediately. Write a letter stating in detail what mistake you have noticed on your credit report and send it via certified mail with a return receipt requested; also enclose a copy of your credit report. By law, you should receive a response from the credit bureau within thirty days. As a matter of interest—in the event a mistake has *not* been made—negative information that appears on your credit report can remain for two to seven years, bankruptcies for up to ten years.

The following is a list of credit bureaus that can provide you with reports of your credit history. They can be contacted via mail, telephone, or through their Internet web sites.

CREDIT BUREAUS IN THE UNITED STATES

✂ Experian,* P.O. Box 2106, Allen, TX 75013-2106; 800-392-1122. ** www.experian.com

---

*Originally known as TRW, which used to offer one free credit report per year. However, Experian discontinued the service in March 1997.

**You are eligible for a free report within sixty days if denied credit, insurance, or employment. You are also eligible for a free report if an apartment rental or checking account is turned down.

✂ Trans Union, P.O. Box 390, Springfield, PA 19064-0390; 312-408-1050. ** www.tuc.com

✂ Equifax, P.O. Box 740241, Atlanta, GA 30374-0241; 800-685-1111. ** www.equifax.com

When seeking a transcript of your credit report, you will most likely need to include a letter with the following: full name, date of birth, Social Security number, names of current and past spouses, current and previous addresses for the past five years, current employer, and signature. A copy of your driver's license might also be required. The usual cost for an individual credit report is between $2 to $8.

When you first get your report it might look very complex. There are usually several pages that will explain how to read the information. It is very important that you examine your credit report carefully since it is a crucial piece of information lenders rely on when you apply for a loan. If you notice any errors, or negative marks that do not coincide with your records, follow the process explained earlier in this section. Want to know more about credit bureaus and how they work? Then check the information below.

Associated Credit Bureaus Inc.

✂ For further information and educational material regarding the Fair Credit Reporting Act and credit bureaus, contact the Associated Credit Bureaus Inc., 1090 Vermont Avenue N.W., Suite 200, Washington, D.C. 20005-4905.

There is further information about credit bureaus on the World Wide Web at www.acb-credit.com. Also, make sure to visit the Federal Trade Commission at www.ftc.gov for information on consumer rights and credit policies.

Keeping your credit report in top shape is important, especially in a country where the word *credit* is so important to a way of life. But sometimes your credit report—as well as other personal accounts—can be negatively affected without any misdoing on your part. To prevent such situations we move on to our next section, "Credit Card Safety and Preparation."

> *It's a good idea to check your credit report a few months before applying for any major loans, such as a home mortgage. This gives you time to clear any errors that you might discover.*

CREDIT CARD SAFETY AND PREPARATION

*The more credit cards you have, the more important it is to read on. The **Joneses** and **Bob** need not only be organized with their credit cards but also prepared and more knowledgeable about proper credit card safety.*

Every time you call customer service in reference to one of your credit cards, they ask you for some security information, such as your mother's maiden name and your Social Security number. It is a good idea for you to have easy access to this security information when transferring balances, checking your account, and especially if your cards ever get lost or stolen. The following is a list of information that you alone should be able to access. It should be kept in a safe place.

FOR YOUR EYES ONLY

✂ Mother's maiden name.
✂ Your Social Security number.
✂ Your date of birth.
✂ Address where your bills are sent.
✂ Your phone number.

If you are also handling accounts for family members or friends, you'll need the same information for each account. In order for you to access their accounts, these individuals will initially need to call the credit card issuer and attach your name to the account. Be sure that the individual designates what type of authorization you have; some credit cards only allow you to review the account, while others require you to be a joint cardholder in order to have access at all.

Because the Joneses have credit card accounts split between them, it is worthwhile and can save much confusion and time for them to have all their accounts under both spouses' names. That way, both spouses need not be around when transferring balances or checking accounts.

Be careful, though, because if you become a joint cardholder, your credit report might ultimately be affected. If it is affected in a negative way, it will be harder for you to get future loans and increases for lines of credit.

In terms of making sure no one else uses your credit card without your authorization, you should review the following guidelines. Most are common sense, but you would be surprised at how many cardholders are not cautious with their credit cards.

FOR YOUR SAFETY

✂ Avoid signing blank receipts.
✂ Void or destroy all carbons and incorrect receipts.

✂ Always draw a line over blank spaces on receipts.

✂ Always save your credit card receipts to compare with billing statements.

✂ Never place your phone number, name, or address on a credit card receipt.

✂ Never write your pin number on your credit card, or anywhere near it. Pin numbers are usually four digits, so they should not be hard to memorize.

✂ Never give your credit card number to anyone over the phone, unless you are dealing with a reputable company and you are the one who made the call.

✂ Sign your credit card as soon as it arrives and destroy the expired card.

Your "The Details" chart will also provide you with a sense of security. If ever you were to have your credit cards lost or stolen, just refer back to this chart, in which you'll have access to all the necessary information in order to make the appropriate cancellations of the accounts involved.

You will find that organizing your security information and knowing how to protect your accounts will help you avoid future frustrations. This is especially important if you plan to travel, which leads us to our next section, "Pack Those Charts."

Ever wonder about placing your personal photo on your credit card? Is it really for your protection? Well, yes, but in actuality, many credit card consumers have a more personal attachment to their credit cards when a photo is on the face of the card. Psychologically, the photo credit card also gives more incentive for keeping the card as opposed to canceling an account, even if the card isn't being used.

PACK THOSE CHARTS!

*The following section is only necessary for those who have many financial responsibilities. The **Joneses** and **Bob**, if they travel frequently, should not consider leaving everything behind, because even on vacation, financial responsibilities follow.*

If you plan on traveling anytime soon, whether for business or pleasure, your debts will still need to be paid. This section applies to those who will be away from home for several weeks at a time. (Weekend travelers, skip ahead to the next section.)

Before embarking on any trip, you need to make a plan for paying your bills, on time, and be sure that there will be enough funds to cover those bills. Many individuals leave personal checks with a friend to be sent before bills are due. This method is fine for one or two bills a month, but if you have numerous bills due each month do not expect your friend to be timely with every bill. You can sometimes send postdated checks to a credit card company, but you must be careful: Most credit card issuers will not be held responsible if for some reason the checks are not credited to your account.

Either method is not recommended, simply because you can put your credit history at risk for ill-timed payments or payments that are not made at all. So how will your bills get paid in your absence? Read on!

HOW TO PAY YOUR BILLS

Today, many banks offer automatic payment services that will pay your bills on time, every month, to any merchant with an address in the United States. Most of the banks are reliable; some even guarantee their services. Find out if your local bank offers such a service, for it will save you time and money in the long run.*

If, besides credit cards, there are other debts you owe—such as mortgages, auto loans, and student loans—some of these payments may be automatically deducted from your checking or savings account by the lender(s). You will have to check with your lender(s) for further information on such services.

The following list explains how to organize your credit card payments before travel if you will be using an institution to pay your bills for you. Even though your bank will be providing instructions, it is best to see firsthand how the process works.

Before Travel

1. Your bank might need several days to set up the auto-payment service (so don't plan on doing this the day before you leave). The first step is for you to call to have them set up the service.
2. Take a look at your "The Details" chart. You will need to organize your credit cards that need to be paid, the last possible closing dates, the amount you wish to pay each card for each month (this figure must be at least the current minimum due!), the payment address that does not require a payment stub, and your account number. Some banks require more, and some require less, information.

---

*Citibank, Chase, and Bank of America are a few of several credit card issuers that offer an automatic payment plan for their credit card holders, in which the minimum due, a fixed amount, or the entire balance is deducted monthly from the cardholder's checking account. This is a great feature when traveling (if you use this service, make a note of it in your "The Details" chart and be aware of the autopayment when transferring balances). Unfortunately, not all credit cards offer this extremely useful feature, but it will soon become a more common service.

3. Next, call the bank back. They will either send you a form or take the required information over the phone. If there are other payments that need to be made, such as utilities, or other debts that other lenders cannot automatically deduct from your account, make sure the proper information is also given.

4. You need to make sure that there are sufficient funds each month in your checking account to cover all payments that will be made. The bank will not make payments if there is no money in your account. (You do not want to access your overdraft account, simply because of the high interest rate.)

5. In the "Pay" column of "The Details" chart, write the amounts that will be paid to each creditor and when they will be paid by your bank.

6. Do not forget that some of your credit cards might have low but temporary interest rates. Make sure that if those particular rates are expiring soon you call requesting that the time period for the interest rate be extended. (Remember "The Words of Power," on page 76?) The last thing you want to have happen is for all those low interest rates to expire when you are away. It is also very troublesome to deal with transferring balances when away.*

7. When you are finally at your destination, you should call each credit card to make sure it has received your payment. It is a good idea to call seven to ten days after the

---

*What is meant by "troublesome" is simply that you would need to contact all the customer service representatives to find out if there are any special interest rates being offered. If a transfer then follows, you'd need to check on it in a few weeks, making sure it'd been processed in both accounts. You would also need to find out the new minimum payments due (or you could figure that out by using the "Monthly Minimum Configurations" information in your "The Details" chart). You would then have to contact your bank and change the amounts automatically being paid to both credit cards. Unless you will be gone for some time, you should try to avoid this situation.

payments are sent from your bank. Remember that you can always call collect if you are calling from out of the country. (NOTE: This step is not absolutely necessary as long as your bank's services are reliable.)

Following these steps might seem time-consuming at first, but they will save you numerous headaches in the future. They definitely made planning Bob's vacation to Florida a whole lot easier.

Remember, it is people who plan ahead who usually win credit card battles. If your bank does not offer such services, you might want to consider switching banks.

We now move to the next section, "Know Your Rights," a vital source of information, especially for those who use credit cards in their everyday lives

KNOW YOUR RIGHTS

*Whether you use your credit cards once a week or once a year, you should be familiar with your rights when using them. This section applies to **all individuals**.*

It is important in life to know your rights, and when it comes to credit cards, that important rule applies double. When you receive a new credit card it will often be accompanied by several pages of your rights and regulations as they apply to the use of the credit card. Rights and regulations sometimes appear on the back of your monthly statements, but often they are not always written so that the average consumer can easily understand them. Here are the most important rights with which you should be familiar.

The Seven Rules

Unauthorized Charges

✄ When using a credit card, your liability depends on how quickly you report any unauthorized charges. Generally speaking, if you notify your credit card issuer within two days, you will not be liable for more than $50; a sixty-day notice, and your maximum liability is $500; any notice given thereafter might result in an unlimited liability on your part. With a debit card, the terms are slightly different. Debit card holders are liable for only $50 for any unauthorized charge, with no notification time period (though it's best to notify the card issuer as soon as the card is missing or stolen). Visa holders are not liable for any unauthorized charges if they notify their credit card issuer within two days, otherwise their liability is $50 thereafter.

Credit for Your Payments

✄ Any payment you make to a credit card should be credited the day it was received, unless the amount falls short of the minimum payment, or any delay on the credit card issuer's part does not cause additional charges for you.

Credit for Annual Fee

✄ In order to avoid paying any annual fee, the credit card holder must notify the credit card issuer within forty days of receiving any statement including an annual fee, if he or she wishes to cancel the credit card and avoid paying the annual fee.

Disputing with Merchant

✂ If a problem ever occurs between you and a merchant and no compromise can be met through good faith, you may delay payment to your credit card for the amount in dispute and any other charges that may apply. You may delay payment as long as the credit card was not issued by the same merchant that you are in dispute with, the purchase was made in your home, or if out of state, within 100 miles of your billing address, and the amount exceeds $50. If the purchase was made farther than those 100 miles away and exceeded $50, or was on a credit card represented by the merchant, you may choose to file action in a small claims court.

Refunds and Credits

✂ If you ever return a purchase or pay more than you owe, you may request a refund from the credit card issuer or keep the credit on your balance. The amount must exceed $1 and the credit card issuer must send you a refund (if you request) within seven business days.

Errors in Your Statement

✂ If there is an error in your monthly statement, you must contact the credit card issuer within sixty days of receiving the statement. If the credit card issuer needs to review the problem, you do not have to pay the amount in question during the period of the review. The credit card issuer must respond to your inquiry within two billing cycles and not after ninety days of receiving your request.

Handing Over Information

✂ Merchants are not allowed to ask you for the following information when you are using a credit card for payment: phone number, address, and driver's license information. Nor are they allowed to ask for your credit card number in the event you are paying for a purchase with a personal check.

There you have it: seven simple rules and rights that you should be familiar with. When dealing with a situation or problem involving your credit card, it helps to accompany any phone request with a letter to the credit card issuer explaining your situation in detail. Remember to handle the situation in a calm and relaxed manner. Avoid calling a customer service representative and raising your voice if something is wrong. Nor should you be defensive in your letter. You will see that by being polite and courteous, your odds of successfully handling whatever situation you are in will increase.

> *Rule of thumb: Always keep all notices, letters, and monthly statements sent to you by your creditors. If you are ever in dispute over a transaction, those pieces of paper might just help you win your defense.*

Additionally, there are several laws that are designed to protect consumers from illegal actions to cardholders. If you would like further information on your rights as a consumer, you may request the "Consumer Protection Booklet" from the Attorney General's Public Protection Division. The toll-free number is 800-441-2555.

By now you should not only be a wiser cardholder but also a more secure one. As proven throughout this book—and more so in this chapter—credit cards aren't just pieces of plastic; they can affect your credit history, they can be targets for those who wish to misuse them, and they can be a form of protection for those whose rights have been violated. With this newly learned information, we will now make the final strategic move, which leads us to the last chapter, "Some Final Comments."

Some Final Comments

A QUICK REVIEW

Throughout the book, **Tom**, **Jennifer**, *the* **Joneses**, *and* **Bob** *have had differences in their battles against their credit card debt. Now they have something in common: They all are soon-to-be victors in winning their credit card wars!*

Chances are you've learned quite a bit so far from the information provided in this book. I hope that you've picked up some useful tricks here and there, and that you've reduced the cost of your debt significantly. Even though you've come this far and might consider yourself a credit card expert, it will not hurt to do a quick review of the key processes in reducing your credit card debt.

POLISH THOSE SKILLS

Organize Your Credit Cards

✂ The first step is to organize your credit cards, statements, special offers, and any correspondence you have received regarding your credit cards. Throw out anything that is expired or simply of no use. Remember how important it is to stay organized throughout the process of getting yourself out of credit card debt.

Don't let the credit card companies take advantage of you because you were unorganized; let's make it a fair fight! In actuality, the sides have evened out, since this book has armed you with the necessary ammunition to not only fight but win the war against credit card debt.

Fill in the Charts

✂ Next, fill in the information required for the charts. Make sure the information is accurate and that you call customer service if you're uncertain about any aspects. "The Layout" chart is the most vital. You will be using it the most often, and it will be a great factor in helping you control the cost of your debt. It is very important that this chart is kept accurate and up-to-date, and that it is completed before reading on.

Determine Your Situation

✂ Analyze your credit cards by using "The Layout" chart. Find out your total debt, your flexibility rating, and the total cost of your debt (AIR), and categorize your credit cards accordingly by interest rates. It is important to know where you stand, which credit cards are the most costly, and which ones to deal with first. Remember that credit card interest rates change; therefore, what is not a priority today might become one.

Make the First Move

✂ Take a look at any offers you have received and determine if there are any you should follow up on. Then call the credit card issuer for any special offers. If nothing is being offered, call the credit card issuer on your terms, using "The Words of Power." You will then have made the first move in greatly reducing the cost of your debt. This process can be time-consuming at first, but once you become familiar with it, it will be just like second nature to you.

Update the Charts

✂ Once you have transferred any balances (do not forget to make note of your transfers in your "The Transfer" chart), your average interest rate on all your credit cards will be going down. Now you must keep all the charts up-to-date. Return to "The Layout" chart and update your new balances, new interest rates, and new expiration dates. You may now relax a bit, knowing that the cost of your debt has been reduced significantly, but don't forget to stay on your toes!

The Payments

✂ Set up a system to pay a fixed amount every month, as explained in "Minimum Payment—Tricks of The Trade," on page 85. Remember not to fall for any of the credit card issuers' tricks, such as the opportunity to skip minimum payments or pay only the minimum due each month. Remember, you can play their games—but play by your rules, not theirs!

Watch Those Fees

✂ Watch your credit limit, annual fees, payments, and possible reasons for penalty fees. You do not want to be penalized or pay more than you should. Just because credit card issuers can make millions from other cardholders doesn't mean you have to contribute. Stay organized and in control!

Be on Your Toes

✂ Make sure to track your credit cards every four to five weeks. If an interest rate is about to expire, be prepared to extend the rate or transfer the balance. The last thing you want is for a credit card company to trap you with high interest rates. Not only should you always make the first move, you should plan on the next few moves: If you have several credit cards whose interest rates will soon expire, you'll want to be prepared for dealing with each one.

The Evaluation

✂ Check your credit history every eight to twelve months to make sure everything is being reported properly. All your work and effort should not go unnoticed. A great benefit in tackling and organizing your credit card debt is that your credit history will prosper from it. Remember that having a spotless credit report will help you in the long run financially.

You can now congratulate yourself for not only fighting the battle against credit cards but nearly winning the war! And yes, you have nearly won the war, because you now have been armed with the knowledge and the know-how to handle and conquer your credit card debt for years to come. There are just a few more things I would like to mention before you celebrate your victory.

WHAT TO DO WHEN OUT OF DEBT

Now that the victims have become victors, changes need to be made. **Tom** *and* **Jennifer** *should each keep one credit* *card with a low credit limit, and use it responsibly to help build their credit history. The **Joneses** and **Bob** should get rid of all their credit cards and consider getting debit cards. And—oh, yes—Bob should **retire**.*

Chances are you will still have some credit card debt by the time you finish this book, so it's a good idea to keep the book handy for the moment when you are finally *free* of debt! That is the time to refer to the following for some important reminders.

THE LIFE AFTER

Get a Debit Card

✂ Remember that you were told to keep your credit cards, even if they had a zero balance? Since you are out of debt and will no longer need to make transfers, you should now cancel all your credit cards. Many banks are now offering ATM cards that can be used in place of personal checks and are accepted anywhere Master-Card or Visa is accepted. The ATM cards are otherwise known as "debit cards," and they function like credit cards—with a few big differences: There are no interest rates, and the money is withdrawn directly from your own checking account, which can certainly help to discipline you.* Without the cash, you should not make

---

*One of the main drawbacks of a debit card is that the money is almost immediately withdrawn (depending on the type of transaction, this can take a few seconds or a few days) from the account, so there is no "float" period. The "float" period is the amount of time your money stays in your account between the date you make a purchase and the date the money is withdrawn from the account. The advantage of having a "float" period is that funds in your account can be used for other purposes, such as earning interest or paying other bills.

the purchase. If your bank doesn't offer a debit card, it soon might.

There's a funny twist on the debit card idea: Your overdraft checking account usually operates by providing you with needed reserves when your account is empty but an interest charge then applies (and usually it's very high). What that means is that once you start to use this reserve, your debit card acts just like a credit card! If you find your bank will not be offering a debit card anytime soon, it might be beneficial to keep *one* of your credit cards—as long as you are extremely careful!

With a debit card, Bob will no longer accumulate credit card debt and costly interest rates. His dream vacations will soon become reality.

Spend Wisely

✂ Make sure that when you do use a credit card or debit card, you do not exceed your available income and other financial responsibilities. When it comes to the holidays or special occasions, it is hard not to buy gifts; try to remember that a more expensive gift does not necessarily mean a better gift. Think of something clever instead, and remember that it is the thought—not the gift itself—that counts. It's a good idea to set a limit to the amount you will spend, though so many consumers seem to go beyond such limits. Try to remember that it is simply not worth buying gifts you will be paying for in the months ahead.

Jennifer has now learned an important lesson: that her spending cost her more than she ever thought possible. Now when she goes out with her friends, she leaves her credit card at home.

Don't Let History Repeat Itself

✂ Find out why you were in debt in the first place. Was it going out to dinner almost every night, shopping each weekend, long-distance phone calls, or just, perhaps, the easy access to your credit cards? Whatever it was, try your best not to do it again, or at least not as excessively. Remember that credit card charges should never be more than 10% of your monthly income (depending on other responsibilities, that 10% can fluctuate).

The Joneses used to use their high interest rate cards for many of their regular daily expenses. When the bills came, they would often pay only the minimum due, leading to an unforeseen accumulation of debt, a mistake they vowed never to repeat when they canceled all their credit card accounts.

Open a Savings Account

✂ Start to build a reserve of cash. If you ever need your credit card in case of emergency, at least you will have some money to pay some, if not all, of the charges. A savings account can also introduce you to the important lesson of saving rather than spending.

Now that neither Tom, Jennifer, the Joneses, or Bob is paying interest on credit card debt—which originally ranged from $5 to $635 a month (before applying the rules of this book)—the money they're saving can go into a savings account, CD, or favorite stock.

Trash That Mail

✂ No matter how hard the temptation, you should never accept any offer sent to you from a credit card company ever again! When the offers come in, just throw them away. Remember that this is exactly how they lured you the first time, so don't let them trap you again.

Since Tom is a credit card issuer's favorite, he has learned of their evils, so to prevent temptation he has already contacted his postmaster to make sure he receives no *unsolicited* mail.*

Last but not least, remember that a credit card is a loan, and often a long-term one. Unfortunately, the temptations provided by credit cards might prove too powerful for some cardholders, so if ever you find yourself losing the credit card battle once more, the next section is meant for you.

THE ADVENTURE CONTINUES ONLINE

*Using the Internet for further help is highly recommended for all readers. Whether you are like **Tom**, who has years of experience using computers and the Internet, or like **Bob**, who is just starting to learn, accessing the Internet can prove very beneficial.*

Much of the information in these pages can be referred to over and over, making them an essential resource in battling credit card debt. An additional feature of this book that sets it apart from other books is that it provides ongoing help to any readers who have access to the Internet. Through accessing my Internet web site, you will find up-to-date information and innumerable suggestions on how to handle your

---

*In the event you are continuously receiving pre-approved offers, you can contact all three credit bureaus (Experian, Trans Union, and Equifax) and ask that they no longer provide information to those who seek it. This will definitely lessen the pile of questionable offers in your mailbox.

credit card debt. Think of www.creditcardfreedom.com as your personal guide—there to help you twenty-four hours a day. The following is a list of some of the information you will find at the web site.

WWW.CREDITCARDFREEDOM.COM

- ✂ What's New in the Credit Card World
- ✂ Top Overall Best Credit Cards
- ✂ Which Credit Card Is Best for You
- ✂ Online Credit Card Applications
- ✂ Suggestions on Reducing Your Debt
- ✂ Links to Useful Web Sites

The Internet web site is continuously changing and growing. Its frequently updated information is provided to help you reduce and manage your credit card debt. That's why I strongly suggest you visit the site for additional guidance in handling your credit cards.

Wait! Don't use *scissors* on your credit cards yet! You might want to read the next section before you take such actions.

SCISSORS ARE TOO CRUEL

Credit cards can make life simpler and easier or more complicated and difficult, depending on how you use them. Chances are you already know how they fit into your lifestyle, so follow the guidelines and suggestions in this book and reap the rewards. The money you'll save will far exceed the cost of this book.

The battle against credit card debt can be a struggle at first, but after reading this book you've increased your odds tenfold toward winning that war. Most important, you've learned some valuable information. By being able to control your credit card debt, you have learned techniques that will be very useful and profitable when dealing with other types of loans. Credit cards themselves can also be good teachers in debt management, for those who learn from their unfortunate experiences most often do not make the same mistakes with other more important loans, such as home mortgages and equity loans.

As you pay off your credit cards, they should be unaccessible, so you do not have the temptation to use them. Put them in a box where they will be safe and out of reach. When you are finally out of credit card debt, take all the credit cards and put them in a picture frame instead of cutting them in half. Then hang the frame somewhere so you will always have interesting dinner conversation to bring up. It will be like a diploma from college, because you will have graduated from credit card debt and you should be congratulated. So until that gratifying moment . . . the best of luck!

> *A common practice for those who've won the credit card battle is to put their cards in a bowl of water and place it in the freezer. Well, this is not recommended—(especially if you have limited freezer space) because if and when the bowl is removed, the ice melts . . . and spending havoc ensues.*

By the way, you might be surprised by the positive changes in our characters' credit card debts, accomplished through the suggestions and methods provided by this book, but you will definitely be even more surprised by the choices and changes they've made in their lives. Take a look at the next section, which provides a detailed look at how Tom, Jennifer, the Joneses, and Bob ultimately took control of and conquered their credit card debt.

FIVE SMILING FACES

The methods and suggestions provided by this book proved to be money-saving techniques for all the characters who implemented them. Not only did they lower the cost of their debt and use different methods to reduce their balances, they also achieved another perspective on how to handle their finances in the future.

Let's take a look at each one and how they did it. (The figures provided here were calculated from the time the individuals had finished reading this book.)

Tom, the student, realized that he had to be careful with his credit cards. Many of his friends saw their credit cards as "tools of freedom," but Tom saw otherwise and took the other road, one that had no deceptions.

Though he had only $319.76 in debt, he knew that that figure could increase, especially if his parents decided to lower his monthly income. He first transferred the balance to his second card at a special 5.9% rate for six months, which lowered his monthly finance charges from $4.60 to $1.49. The minimum due each month was $10, so he then decided to get a part-time job, which contributed an additional $30 a month to his credit cards.

He was able to get out of credit card debt in nine months, a definite triumph for someone who was bombarded by credit card offers in the mail. The part-time job also offered Tom the financial freedom he desired. After nine months he canceled one of his credit cards, keeping the other for an emergency and grocery shopping (to help build his credit history and accumulate frequent flyer miles). He now gives advice to his fellow students on how to properly manage their credit cards.

Not Applying the Rules of Credit Card Debt . . .

Original Balance:	$319.76
Average Interest Rate:	18.40%
Monthly Contribution:	Minimum Due
Balance (after one year):	$259.18
Total Interest Paid (after one year):	$53.39

Applying the Rules of Credit Card Debt . . .

Original Balance:	$319.76
Average Interest Rate (after one month):	5.9%
Monthly Contribution:	$40.00
Balance (after nine months):	$0.00
Total Interest Paid (after nine months):	$10.72*

Jennifer, the extra spender, eventually learned to spend less. Since she was not able to increase her income, her next alternative and wisest decision was to budget.

By lowering her interest rates to an average 7.18% and cutting unnecessary expenses (contributing some money to her credit cards), she was able to reduce her credit card debt by over 66% in one year. Not bad for someone who likes to spend money! As her debt decreased, she started to consider alternative uses for the money she was saving—and no, it was not for new shoes.

In fact, she opened a brokerage account and started to invest in stocks and bonds. She did so well that she made more than enough money in nine months to cover the money

---

*After receiving the billing statement with the balance of $319.76 and transferring it, Tom still had to pay one month at 18.40% before receiving the special 5.9% rate from his other credit card. Otherwise, his total interest paid would have only been $7.24 for the nine months.

she lost in finance charges over the previous two years with her credit cards. And she learned an important lesson: Making money can be almost as much fun as spending it. So what happened to her credit cards? She eventually canceled most of her accounts (keeping one with a very *low* credit limit), and kept the canceled cards around to remind herself of those many, many shoe stores.

Not Applying the Rules of Credit Card Debt . . .

Original Balance:	$5,810.55
Average Interest Rate:	18.72%
Monthly Contribution:	Minimum Due
Balance (after one year):	$5,516.55
Total Interest Paid (after one year):	$1,060.12

Applying the Rules of Credit Card Debt . . .

Original Balance:	$5,810.55
Average Interest Rate (after one month):	10%
Average Interest Rate (after two months)	7.18%
Monthly Contribution:	$400.00*
Balance (after one year):	$1,928.45
Total Interest Paid (after one year):	$355.63

The **Joneses**, the next-door neighbors, had to look long and hard to truly reduce the burden of their credit card debt. They realized that many of the alternatives available to most were unavailable to them, since they were busy with their jobs and children and had already been living on a tight bud-

---

*Since the extra funds resulted from Jennifer's budgeted expenses, her savings of $400 could not apply to her credit card payments until the second month after she implemented her debt-reduction plan.

get. Consolidation seemed attractive at first, but they realized after adding the closing costs and higher interest rates that they'd put off applying for a loan until their financial circumstances called for it.

So they did what most *savvy* credit card holders do: They lowered the average interest rate on their credit cards to 6.9% and considerably reduced their debt by paying more than the minimum due.

They also realized that their savings account was only returning 3% on their funds. Because they had to pay taxes on those earnings, the actual return was less, so they decided to contribute from their savings account to their credit card debt on a monthly basis. By applying a consistent $1,100 a month (on average $250 more than the total minimums due per month in the first year), they were able to reduce their debts by almost $9,000 in the first year alone. Eventually, they sold some other assets that were not providing reasonable returns and were able to completely wipe out their credit card debt in slightly less than three years.

The Joneses then canceled all their credit cards and applied for two debit cards; one for him, the other for her. Ultimately, they no longer faced the evils of the minimum payment. In fact, they had a new philosophy: If they couldn't afford it, they wouldn't buy it.

Not Applying the Rules of Credit Card Debt . . .

Original Balance:	$45,127.32
Average Interest Rate:	16.90%
Monthly Contribution:	Minimum Due
Balance (after one year):	$42,145.07
Total Interest Paid (after one year):	$7,371.88

Applying the Rules of Credit Card Debt . . .

Original Balance:	$45,127.32
Average Interest Rate (after one month):	10.2%
Average Interest Rate (after two months):	7.5%
Average Interest Rate (after three months):	6.9%
Monthly Contribution:	$1,100.00
Balance (after one year):	$36,161.74
Total Interest Paid (after one year):	$3,342.34

Bob, the should-be retiree, first needed to overcome the shock of his poor investment decision, then to overcome an additional obstacle: his disorganization in managing his credit card debts.

He never knew the total balance of all his cards, nor how much he was being robbed by an average interest rate of 17.35%. Once he was able to organize and analyze his credit card debt, he took control of the situation. He realized that by lowering his finance charges, applying a consistent fixed amount above the minimum due, and most important, keeping track of all transactions by using the charts provided, he would be free of credit card debt.

After one year of deliberately handling his credit cards and reducing his debt by nearly $4,800, he was able to qualify for a loan that not only offered a discounted one year rate of 6.2% but also provided no additional costs or prepayment penalties. Since the interest was tax deductible and he was planning on paying the rest of the debt within that year, it proved to be a smart choice.

Once he was out of debt, he learned a valuable lesson at his age: that taking high risks can be very consequential, especially when those risks are tied to borrowing from credit cards with very high interest rates.

In conclusion, he decided never to invest money he didn't

have and to invest only in low-risk investments. After placing his money in safe-deposits, he was finally able to take his trip to Florida, and on this trip he preferred to put his new debit card to use rather than use any credit cards.

Not Applying the Rules of Credit Card Debt . . .

Original Balance:	$20,933.97
Average Interest Rate:	17.35%
Monthly Contribution:	Minimum Due
Balance (after one year):	$19,629.20
Total Interest Paid (after one year):	$3,517.24

Applying the Rules of Credit Card Debt . . .

Original Balance:	$20,933.97
Average Interest Rate (after one month):	16.5%
Average Interest Rate (after two months):	12.99%
Average Interest Rate (after three months):	10%
Average Interest Rate (after four months):	6.5%
Monthly Contribution:	$585.00
Balance (after one year):	$16,158.92
Total Interest Paid (after one year):	$1,747.47

Glossary A to Z

✂ **Account Number:** The identification for your credit card account. The number usually consists of sixteen digits split into four categories. The first six numbers determine the company that issued the card, the next four numbers determine the region and branch information of the bank, the following five numbers specify your personal account number, and the last number is usually for security reasons.

✂ **Annual Fee:** Flat yearly charge that is sometimes referred to as a membership or annual membership fee. This paid fee allows the consumer access to the credit card and its privileges.

✂ **APR (annual percentage rate):** Your cost of using the credit; includes the interest and sometimes other charges that might be applied to your account (also referred to as the periodic rate).

✂ **Cash Advance:** Most credit cards offer you the option of taking cash from your credit card. You may do this by using a check or a pin number, up to the available amount of your credit limit. Interest rates tend to be high for cash advances, and often there is a fee for each withdrawal (sometimes simply referred to as advances).

✂ **Charge Card:** A type of credit card (such as American Express) in which payments must be made in full each month and there is no interest applied.

✂ **Closing Date:** This is the date on which your credit card statement closes. The dates are usually consistent every month and appear on each statement. Any purchases or payments made after this date will appear on the following statement.

✂ **Credit Available:** Your credit limit minus your current balance. This determines the amount of credit that can be used. The amount changes as your balance changes.

✂ **Credit Card:** A type of revolving loan (whatever is paid can then be borrowed again) that can be used to make purchases, take cash advances, and arrange balance transfers. If not paid in full within a given time period the amount due will incur interest.

✂ **Credit Limit:** The maximum amount of credit one may access on a credit card. This amount will be on your credit card statement.

✂ **Credit Rating:** Drafted by the credit grantor in terms of the individual's credit worthiness and responsibility in paying past and current debt.

✂ **Credit Report:** Collection of an individual's current and past debt and its maintenance history: timely or late payments. You can obtain your credit report from any of several credit bureau agencies in the United States.

✂ **Daily Periodic Rate:** Simply the annual percentage rate divided by the number of days in a year (sometimes referred to as the daily interest rate).

✂ **Debit Card:** A type of ATM card that withdraws funds directly from your checking account for each purchase that is made with the card. There are no finance charges, and your limit is the amount of money in your checking account.

✂ **Debt Consolidation:** The method of combining all short-term debt (credit cards, auto loans, etc.) into one large loan.

✂ **Finance Charge:** Represents the actual amount of dollars you must pay in fees on the amount of credit used. Usually, it is the interest charge on your debt, but sometimes it includes other fees, such as transfer balance and cash advance fees. There are different methods by which finance charges are figured: either by adjusted balance, average daily balance, or previous balance multiplied by the daily or monthly periodic rate.

✂ **Fixed Interest Rate:** Type of interest rate that is fixed and will not change in relation to fluctuations in other indexes. For example, if the fixed interest rate is 9.5%, it will not change for the time period agreed between the cardholder and the account issuer.

✂ **Grace Period:** Period of time, usually between twenty-five and thirty days, in which one can pay an outstanding balance in full to avoid any finance charges. This applies to balances that are paid in full each month, not to those accounts that carry a revolving balance. Cash advances also do not apply, since interest incurs as soon as those transactions are made.

✂ **Interest Rate:** Varies among credit cards. The interest rate determines the cost of your balance. Some interest rates are determined in relation to the prime rate, some are fixed, and some are determined in relation to the risk of the individual using the card.

✂ **Minimum Payment:** Represents the minimum amount of money you are obligated to pay each month against your credit card balance. The figure is determined by the size of the balance and the formula the lender chooses to use in determining the minimum amount due.

✂ **Monthly Periodic Rate:** The annual percentage rate divided by the number of months in a year.

✂ **Payment Due Date:** The date on which the credit card issuer must receive at least your minimum payment.

✂ **Pre-Approval:** A screening process in which an applicant needs to pass through two stages of approval: general, then specific (when variables such as income, job duration, credit history, etc., come into play).

✂ **Retail Card:** A card issued, generally, by an oil company or a department store. These cards are similar to credit cards, the only exception being that a retail card can be used only to buy the products or services of the company that issued it.

✂ **Secured Credit Card:** A type of credit card in which one must maintain a savings account to secure the line of credit for the card. The savings account generally equals 50% to 100% of the actual line of credit.

✂ **Secured Debt:** A type of debt that is secured by collateral such as a house (a mortgage or a home equity loan) or a car.

✂ **Teaser Rates:** Low interest rates offered by credit card issuers for short periods, usually three to nine months. These low rates are usually offered with an application for a new credit card, although an already active credit card account might also offer such a rate for purchases, balance transfers, and/or cash advances.

✂ **Transaction Fees:** Charges that are applied to your credit card balance by the credit card issuer (cash advance fees, late payment fees, returned payment fees, stopped payment fees, and over-the-credit-limit charges).

✂ **Transfer Checks:** Checks that are offered, either by mail or a telephone call, by the credit card issuer. They can be used only to transfer a balance from another credit card account to the one issuing the checks.

✂ **Unsecured Debt:** Any type of debt that does not involve collateral such as a house or car. Credit cards are considered unsecured debt.

✂ **Variable Interest Rate:** Type of interest rate that fluctuates in accordance with other indexes, such as the prime rate. (For example, if the variable interest rate is related to the prime rate, and the prime rate increases by 2%, so will the variable interest rate.)

SAMPLE STATEMENT — Bank ABC

Detach top portion and return with payment

① Account Number	② New Balance	③ Payment Due Date	④ Minimum Payment Due	⑤ Amount Enclosed
1231-2311-9383-0000	$2,957.53	5/21/97	$59.00	$

John Smith
123 Nowhere Street
East Hampton, NY 11937

⑥ Make check payable to:
Bank ABC
⑦ PO Box 3343
Sioux Falls, SD 65772-3343

⑧ Address Change:

_____
_____
_____
_____

⑨ For Customer Service: call or write 800-898-9833
PO Box 3499, Sioux Falls, SD 65772-3499

Account Number	⑩ Total Credit Line	⑪ Available Credit Line	⑫ Closing Date	Payment Due Date	Minimum Payment Due
1231-2311-9383-0000	$3,500	$542.47	4/26/97	5/21/97	$59.00

⑬ Transaction Date	⑭ Posting Date	⑮ Ref. Number	⑯ Description of Transaction	⑰ Charges	⑱ Credits
3/10	3/12	7334299823DOKDE23	Food Market #223	44.94	
3/14	3/15	6333722342FEFGOO7	Office USA	81.36	
3/17	3/20	7736009232KKSQWP3	Copy Shop #98	10.32	
3/22	3/29	2239133891JUDE08	Cameras International	110.67	
3/28	3/30	223898EED2123CRDW	Sunglasses Are Us		-49.99
			TOTAL	$197.30	

⑲ **AIRLINE REBATE SUMMARY**

Last Month's Balance	5,439
Rebates Earned This Month	247
Rebates Redeemed or Expired	50
Current Balance	5,636

⑳ Previous Balance	㉑ (-) Payments and Credits	㉒ (+) Purchases	㉓ (+) Cash Advances	㉔ (+) Finance Charges	(=) New Balance
$2807.53	$114.99	247.26	$0.00	$17.73	$2957.53

FINANCE CHARGE SCHEDULE

㉕ Category	㉖ Daily Periodic Rate	㉗ Annual Percentage Rate	㉘ Balance Subject to Finance Charges*	㉙ Number of Days in Billing Cycle:
Purchases	.046986%	17.15%	$ 0.00	
Cash Advances	.054246%	19.80%	$ 0.00	**32**
Balance Transfers	.021643%	7.90%	$ 2,692.54	

*See reverse side for important information. (30)

Decoding the Monthly Statement

The sample statement here has been uniquely and carefully constructed to be similar to the most common statements used by credit card issuers in order to offer an informative and legitimate representation.

1. **Account Number:** Simply the identification number of your credit card account.
2. **New Balance:** The amount you currently owe on your credit card after all adjustments are made, such as any new purchases and recent payments.
3. **Payment Due Date:** The credit card company must receive your payment by the posted date. Some companies offer a grace period of a few days after the due date before applying late fees. Depending on your location and the payment destination, it is generally a good idea to send your payment at least six business days before the due date.
4. **Minimum Payment Due:** You must pay at least this amount before the due date. The minimum due is relative to your balance and the manner in which the credit card issuer determines the payment. There are numerous ways of determining the minimum payment, such as 2% of a balance or dividing the balance by 48.
5. **Amount Enclosed:** The amount you are sending is written here. This is useful to the creditor when there is

more than one check being sent at one time (i.e. one payment check and one balance transfer check).

6. **Make check payable to:** The check must be made out to whatever name is given. (Sometimes the intended addressor can be different if you are sending payment without a payment stub. In that case, you would have to contact customer service for the appropriate payee name.)

7. **Payment Address:** This is where your payment will be going. (If the address is in your city, the payment will arrive much faster than if the destination were several states away.)

8. **Address Change:** If, by the next statement you'll receive, you plan to be living somewhere else, or if you notice an error in your mailing address, you need to note it here.

9. **Customer Service:** If you have questions or problems with your account you should contact customer service. Any serious problems should be called in first and then followed up by a letter.

10. **Total Credit Line:** The total amount of money you may borrow from your credit card. Some credit card issuers have different credit limits for purchases and cash advances.

11. **Available Credit Line:** The current amount of credit you have access to for purchases, cash advances, or balance transfers. Once again, there might be different amounts available for either purchases or cash advances.

12. **Closing Date:** Each billing cycle has a closing date. The statement is usually printed and sent out on that date. Any transactions made after the closing date will appear on the following statement. Closing dates might or might not occur on the same date each month.

13. **Transaction Date:** The date on which you used the card will be in this column. When you are checking the dates on your receipts against the dates on your statement, look to the "Transaction Date" column.

14. **Posting Date:** The date on which a transaction you made with the credit card was posted to your account. The date is usually several days after the actual transaction was made. The difference between the posting and transaction dates can vary between merchants and credit card issuers.

15. **Reference Number:** A tracking system used between the bank and the merchant. If the bank needs to, it is also able to verify the type of transactions you have been making with the credit card for marketing purposes from those reference numbers. (For example, if you have been making numerous balance transfers to other credit cards, the reference number might end with the letter *T*, something the bank will look for.)

16. **Description of Transaction:** A short description or abbreviation of where you made a transaction or the type of transaction it was.

17. **Charges:** In this column you will see the dollar amount for each transaction you made with the credit card. Finance charges, such as cash advance or late fees, might also be posted in this column.

18. **Credits:** Any amount that is credited to your account—your previous payment and any merchandise purchased with the credit card and recently returned—will be posted in this column. Some statements have only one column for charges and credits, and in such cases the credits are shown with a minus sign (–).

19. **Airline Rebate Summary:** If you are earning benefits, such as points toward free purchases, your credit card might display your current status with the program

somewhere on your statement every month. Any new purchases made will increase your points, and any returned merchandise or expired points will reduce your points. Such a monthly reminder helps keep the customer informed of his or her benefits, while encouraging the individual to use the card.

20. **Previous Balance:** This is simply the balance that had been posted on your previous statement as the "New Balance."

21. **Payments and Credits:** Any payments or credits that were made and posted to the account after the closing date of the previous statement and before the closing date of this statement will appear in this box.

22. **Purchases:** Any purchases that were made and posted to the account after the closing date of the previous statement and before the closing date of this statement will appear in this box.

23. **Cash Advances:** Any cash advance that was made and posted to the account after the closing date of the previous statement and before the closing date of this statement will appear in this box. Cash advances can include ATM withdrawals as well as balance transfers.

24. **Finance Charges:** New finance charges are applied to your previous balance and to any new cash advances. As long as you have a grace period for new purchases, there will be no finance charges for new purchases. Finance charges represent fees for using the credit card such as interest, cash advances, and late payment fees.

25. **Category:** There are usually different interest rates for different transactions made with your credit card. Most transactions are categorized in one of three categories: purchases, cash advances, and balance transfers.

26. **Daily Periodic Rate:** Listed here are different daily interest rates for each of the categories listed. The daily

periodic rate is figured by taking the annual percentage rate and dividing by the number of days in a year.

27. **Annual Percentage Rate:** There are different annual interest rates for each of the categories listed. Depending on specific promotions or types of credit cards, certain categories will have higher interest rates than others. Cash advances will usually have the highest interest rates, and balance transfers the lowest.

28. **Balance Subject to Finance Charges:** The exact dollar amount that is being applied to each interest rate. If you have made several purchases, cash advances, and perhaps a balance transfer with the credit card, the dollar amount of each transaction would be placed in this column accordingly.

29. **Number of Days in Billing Cycle:** This is otherwise known as the grace period. The number of days shown is the number of days in which you must pay off the new balance to avoid having finance charges apply in the next statement. The same rule applies for new purchases; as long as they are paid within the number of days specified there will be no interest applied to them in the next statement.

30. **See reverse side for important information:** You will find detailed information concerning your account in fine print. Whether it's a description of terms and your rights, or answers to questions you might have, this is the place where the credit card company provides certain information required by law.

IT'S NOT JUST PLASTIC

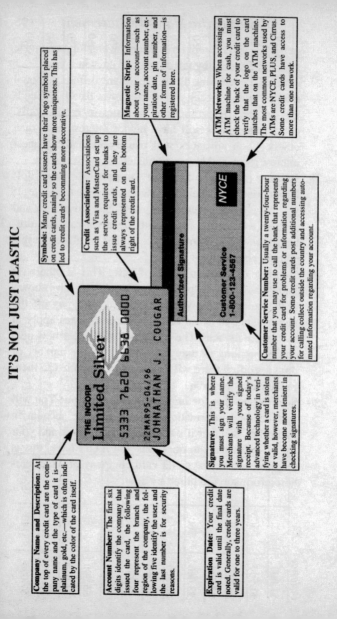

Company Name and Description: At the top of every credit card are the company name and the type of card it is—platinum, gold, etc.—which is often indicated by the color of the card itself.

Symbols: Many credit card issuers have their logo symbols placed on credit cards, mainly so the cards show more uniqueness. This has led to credit cards' becomming more decorative.

Credit Associations: Associations such as Visa and MasterCard set up the service required for banks to issue credit cards, and they are always represented on the bottom right of the credit card.

Magnetic Strip: Information about your account—such as your name, account number, expiration date, pin number, and other forms of information—is registered here.

ATM Networks: When accessing an ATM machine for cash, you must check the back of your credit card to verify that the logo on the card matches that on the ATM machine. The most common networks used by ATMs are NYCE, PLUS, and Cirrus. Some credit cards have access to more than one network.

Account Number: The first six digits identify the company that issued the card, the following four represent the branch and region of the company, the following five identify the user, and the last number is for security reasons.

Expiration Date: Your credit card is valid until the final date noted. Generally, credit cards are valid for one to three years.

Signature: This is where you must sign your name. Merchants will verify the signature with your signed receipt. Because of today's advanced technology in verifying whether a card is stolen or valid, however, merchants have become more lenient in checking signatures.

Customer Service Number: Usually a twenty-four-hour number that you may use to call the bank that represents your credit card for problems or information regarding your account. Some credit cards post additional numbers for calling collect outside the country and accessing automated information regarding your account.

INTEREST COMPARISON CHART

Balance	2%	3%	4%	5%	6%	7%	8%	9%	10%	11%	12%
$1,000	$20	$30	$40	$50	$60	$70	$80	$90	$100	$110	$120
$1,500	$30	$45	$60	$75	$90	$105	$120	$135	$150	$165	$180
$2,000	$40	$60	$80	$100	$120	$140	$160	$180	$200	$220	$240
$2,500	$50	$75	$100	$125	$150	$175	$200	$225	$250	$275	$300
$3,000	$60	$90	$120	$150	$180	$210	$240	$270	$300	$330	$360
$3,500	$70	$105	$140	$175	$210	$245	$280	$315	$350	$385	$420
$4,000	$80	$120	$160	$200	$240	$280	$320	$360	$400	$440	$480
$4,500	$90	$135	$180	$225	$270	$315	$360	$405	$450	$495	$540
$5,000	$100	$150	$200	$250	$300	$350	$400	$450	$500	$550	$600
$5,500	$110	$165	$220	$275	$330	$385	$440	$495	$550	$605	$660
$6,000	$120	$180	$240	$300	$360	$420	$480	$540	$600	$660	$720
$6,500	$130	$195	$260	$325	$390	$455	$520	$585	$650	$715	$780
$7,000	$140	$210	$280	$350	$420	$490	$560	$630	$700	$770	$840

INTEREST COMPARISON CHART (continued)

Balance	2%	3%	4%	5%	6%	7%	8%	9%	10%	11%	12%
$7,500	$150	$225	$300	$375	$450	$525	$600	$675	$750	$825	$900
$8,000	$160	$240	$320	$400	$480	$560	$640	$720	$800	$880	$960
$8,500	$170	$255	$340	$425	$510	$595	$680	$765	$850	$935	$1,020
$9,000	$180	$270	$360	$450	$540	$630	$720	$810	$900	$990	$1,080
$9,500	$190	$285	$380	$475	$570	$665	$760	$855	$950	$1,045	$1,140
$10,000	$200	$300	$400	$500	$600	$700	$800	$900	$1,000	$1,100	$1,200
$10,500	$210	$315	$420	$525	$630	$735	$840	$945	$1,050	$1,155	$1,260
$11,000	$220	$330	$440	$550	$660	$770	$880	$990	$1,100	$1,210	$1,320
$11,500	$230	$345	$460	$575	$690	$805	$920	$1,035	$1,150	$1,265	$1,380
$12,000	$240	$360	$480	$600	$720	$840	$960	$1,080	$1,200	$1,320	$1,440
$12,500	$250	$375	$500	$625	$750	$875	$1,000	$1,125	$1,250	$1,375	$1,500
$13,000	$260	$390	$520	$650	$780	$910	$1,040	$1,170	$1,300	$1,430	$1,560
$13,500	$270	$405	$540	$675	$810	$945	$1,080	$1,215	$1,350	$1,485	$1,620
$14,000	$280	$420	$560	$700	$840	$980	$1,120	$1,260	$1,400	$1,540	$1,680

$14,500	$290	$435	$580	$725	$870	$1,015	$1,160	$1,305	$1,450	$1,595	$1,740
$15,000	$300	$450	$600	$750	$900	$1,050	$1,200	$1,350	$1,500	$1,650	$1,800
$15,500	$310	$465	$620	$775	$930	$1,085	$1,240	$1,395	$1,550	$1,705	$1,860
$16,000	$320	$480	$640	$800	$960	$1,120	$1,280	$1,440	$1,600	$1,760	$1,920
$16,500	$330	$495	$660	$825	$990	$1,155	$1,320	$1,485	$1,650	$1,815	$1,980
$17,000	$340	$510	$680	$850	$1,020	$1,190	$1,360	$1,530	$1,700	$1,870	$2,040
$17,500	$350	$525	$700	$875	$1,050	$1,225	$1,400	$1,575	$1,750	$1,925	$2,100
$18,000	$360	$540	$720	$900	$1,080	$1,260	$1,440	$1,620	$1,800	$1,980	$2,160
$18,500	$370	$555	$740	$925	$1,110	$1,295	$1,480	$1,665	$1,850	$2,035	$2,220
$19,000	$380	$570	$760	$950	$1,140	$1,330	$1,520	$1,710	$1,900	$2,090	$2,280
$19,500	$390	$585	$780	$975	$1,170	$1,365	$1,560	$1,755	$1,950	$2,145	$2,340
$20,000	$400	$600	$800	$1,000	$1,200	$1,400	$1,600	$1,800	$2,000	$2,200	$2,400

INTEREST COMPARISON CHART

Balance	13%	14%	15%	16%	17%	18%	19%	20%	21%	22%	23%
$1,000	$130	$140	$150	$160	$170	$180	$190	$200	$210	$220	$230
$1,500	$195	$210	$225	$240	$255	$270	$285	$300	$315	$330	$345
$2,000	$260	$280	$300	$320	$340	$360	$380	$400	$420	$440	$460
$2,500	$325	$350	$375	$400	$425	$450	$475	$500	$525	$550	$575
$3,000	$390	$420	$450	$480	$510	$540	$570	$600	$630	$660	$690
$3,500	$455	$490	$525	$560	$595	$630	$665	$700	$735	$770	$805
$4,000	$520	$560	$600	$640	$680	$720	$760	$800	$840	$880	$920
$4,500	$585	$630	$675	$720	$765	$810	$855	$900	$945	$990	$1,035
$5,000	$650	$700	$750	$800	$850	$900	$950	$1,000	$1,050	$1,100	$1,150
$5,500	$715	$770	$825	$880	$935	$990	$1,045	$1,100	$1,155	$1,210	$1,265
$6,000	$780	$840	$900	$960	$1,020	$1,080	$1,140	$1,200	$1,260	$1,320	$1,380
$6,500	$845	$910	$975	$1,040	$1,105	$1,170	$1,235	$1,300	$1,365	$1,430	$1,495
$7,000	$910	$980	$1,050	$1,120	$1,190	$1,260	$1,330	$1,400	$1,470	$1,540	$1,610
$7,500	$975	$1,050	$1,125	$1,200	$1,275	$1,350	$1,425	$1,500	$1,575	$1,650	$1,725
$8,000	$1,040	$1,120	$1,200	$1,280	$1,360	$1,440	$1,520	$1,600	$1,680	$1,760	$1,840

$8,500	$1,105	$1,190	$1,275	$1,360	$1,445	$1,530	$1,615	$1,700	$1,785	$1,870	$1,955
$9,000	$1,170	$1,260	$1,350	$1,440	$1,530	$1,620	$1,710	$1,800	$1,890	$1,980	$2,070
$9,500	$1,235	$1,330	$1,425	$1,520	$1,615	$1,710	$1,805	$1,900	$1,995	$2,090	$2,185
$10,000	$1,300	$1,400	$1,500	$1,600	$1,700	$1,800	$1,900	$2,000	$2,100	$2,200	$2,300
$10,500	$1,365	$1,470	$1,575	$1,680	$1,785	$1,890	$1,995	$2,100	$2,205	$2,310	$2,415
$11,000	$1,430	$1,540	$1,650	$1,760	$1,870	$1,980	$2,090	$2,200	$2,310	$2,420	$2,530
$11,500	$1,495	$1,610	$1,725	$1,840	$1,955	$2,070	$2,185	$2,300	$2,415	$2,530	$2,645
$12,000	$1,560	$1,680	$1,800	$1,920	$2,040	$2,160	$2,280	$2,400	$2,520	$2,640	$2,760
$12,500	$1,625	$1,750	$1,875	$2,000	$2,125	$2,250	$2,375	$2,500	$2,625	$2,750	$2,875
$13,000	$1,690	$1,820	$1,950	$2,080	$2,210	$2,340	$2,470	$2,600	$2,730	$2,860	$2,990
$13,500	$1,755	$1,890	$2,025	$2,160	$2,295	$2,430	$2,565	$2,700	$2,835	$2,970	$3,105
$14,000	$1,820	$1,960	$2,100	$2,240	$2,380	$2,520	$2,660	$2,800	$2,940	$3,080	$3,220
$14,500	$1,885	$2,030	$2,175	$2,320	$2,465	$2,610	$2,755	$2,900	$3,045	$3,190	$3,335
$15,000	$1,950	$2,100	$2,250	$2,400	$2,550	$2,700	$2,850	$3,000	$3,150	$3,300	$3,450
$15,500	$2,015	$2,170	$2,325	$2,480	$2,635	$2,790	$2,945	$3,100	$3,255	$3,410	$3,565
$16,000	$2,080	$2,240	$2,400	$2,560	$2,720	$2,880	$3,040	$3,200	$3,360	$3,520	$3,680

INTEREST COMPARISON CHART (continued)

Balance	13%	14%	15%	16%	17%	18%	19%	20%	21%	22%	23%
$16,500	$2,145	$2,310	$2,475	$2,640	$2,805	$2,970	$3,135	$3,300	$3,465	$3,630	$3,795
$17,000	$2,210	$2,380	$2,550	$2,720	$2,890	$3,060	$3,230	$3,400	$3,570	$3,740	$3,910
$17,500	$2,275	$2,450	$2,625	$2,800	$2,975	$3,150	$3,325	$3,500	$3,675	$3,850	$4,025
$18,000	$2,340	$2,520	$2,700	$2,880	$3,060	$3,240	$3,420	$3,600	$3,780	$3,960	$4,140
$18,500	$2,405	$2,590	$2,750	$2,960	$3,145	$3,330	$3,515	$3,700	$3,885	$4,070	$4,255
$19,000	$2,470	$2,660	$2,850	$3,040	$3,230	$3,420	$3,610	$3,800	$3,990	$4,180	$4,370
$19,500	$2,535	$2,730	$2,925	$3,120	$3,315	$3,510	$3,705	$3,900	$4,095	$4,290	$4,485
$20,000	$2,600	$2,800	$3,000	$3,200	$3,400	$3,600	$3,800	$4,000	$4,200	$4,400	$4,600

ALEXANDER DASKALOFF's interest in personal finance began when investing in comic books at age ten. At sixteen, he began trading stocks and at eighteen received his first credit card. Upon college graduation, he conducted a one year study on the use of credit cards by American consumers, resulting in *Credit Card Debt: Reduce Your Financial Burden in Three Easy Steps*. He currently lives in East Hampton, New York.

The Best in Biographies

HAVE A NICE DAY!
A Tale of Blood and Sweatsocks
by Mankind

0-06-103101-1/$7.99 US/$10.99 Can

THE ROCK SAYS
by The Rock

0-06-103116-X/$7.99 US/$10.99 Can

JACK AND JACKIE:
Portrait of an American Marriage
by Christopher Andersen

0-380-73031-6/$6.99 US/$8.99 Can

CELINE DION:
MY STORY, MY DREAM
by Celine Dion

0-380-81905-8/ $7.99 US

CYBILL DISOBEDIENCE
by Cybill Shepherd and Aimee Lee Ball

0-06-103014-7/ $7.50 US/ $9.99 Can

WALK THIS WAY:
The Autobiography of Aerosmith
by Aerosmith, with Stephen Davis

0-380-79531-0/ $7.99 US/ $9.99 Can

EINSTEIN: THE LIVES AND TIMES
by Ronald W. Clark

0-380-01159-X/$7.99 US/$10.99 Can

I, TINA *by Tina Turner and Kurt Loder*

0-380-70097-2/ $6.99 US/ $9.99 Can

....